The book provides meaningful tools for any aspiring 'wave maker' to take charge and embody the change they want to see in the world. **Make Waves** empowers readers to become everyday leaders by enacting real change in their lives, communities and businesses. You'll find this book provides meaningful tools for any aspiring 'wave maker' to take charge and embody the change they want to see in the world.

– Doug Conant
coauthor of the NYT bestseller Touchpoints, founder of
Conant Leadership & former CEO of Campbell Soup and
President of Nabisco Foods

Make Waves is a pragmatic, inspiring must-read for any leader or professional who wants to drive meaningful change at work or in life. It's full of practical guidance and examples that you can learn from and apply to your change.

– Rusty Shelton
best-selling author, keynote Speaker, and founder of Zilker Media

Make Waves provides a unique and incredibly motivating approach to taking on change. Change, no matter how large or small, personal or professional, can seem daunting and Patti's book causes you to think that you can make a difference in a meaningful way. Patti's guidance causes you to step back, think, and get inspired to act. The book is just the right amount of how-to and inspiration. A must read!

– Maria Cramer
Head of Corporate Professional Services Thomson Reuters

In **Make Waves**, Patti Johnson answers the question, "What is leadership?" Her writing is filled with stories and examples of real leaders and real leadership. This is a must-read for anyone who has a wave that he or she needs to make!

– Larry Peters
former professor of Management & Leadership Development,
Neeley School of Business, Texas Christian University (TCU)

Make Waves is a wonderful narrative on change and how to most effectively navigate through it, with both real-world and practical examples. In a world of increasing change and growing complexity, it serves as a great resource to help manage through both personal and professional changes everyone experiences. It avoids the all-too-common pitfalls of the overly theoretical or academic; rather, it is a great balance of real-world examples that can be applied in all settings.

– David Nashif
former Vice President of Change Leadership, McKesson

Who better from whom to learn the art of change than Patti Johnson, a veteran of management consulting Accenture and a self-made wave maker? Make Waves proves that lighting that match is not just for high-profile people. Each of us has the power and ability to transform our lives, jobs, and organizations in incredible ways.

– Alexandra Levit
Workforce Futurist, WSJ columnist, CEO of Inspiration at Work

In **Make Waves**, Patti Johnson shares pragmatic principles and practical tools to get us started on the journey of leaving a positive legacy wherever we are in the workplace and marketplace.

– K. Shelette Stewart, PhD
Harvard and Stewart Consulting

Want to make a change, but are completely unsure of how to pull it off – or even, maybe, where to start? Drop everything and read Patti Johnson's phenomenal, inspirational book, **Make Waves**. Her formula – Think, Know, Do – is simple without being simplistic. Rather it's the essential 'how-to' manual for those among us who thirst to bring needed change to our teams, our organizations, our communities, or maybe even our world. Savor every page. Scribble your notes. Read, plan, act. Make your own waves!

– Ted Coine
CEO of Benevolent Capital Group, author

Make Waves is a fun and informative book that challenges each of us to find places in our lives where we can be positively disruptive. There are a lot of business books that provide great theories and models for personal change and transformation, but Patti Johnson is able to transition from the conceptual to practical and demonstrates how everyday individuals found the power to bring positive change to their work, schools, and communities. This book serves as a reminder that everyone can move from being a spectator to an active participant in bringing about positive change. A great read for everyone from corporate leaders, early career individuals, and students.

– Miya Maysent
former Vice President, 7-Eleven, Inc.

Make Waves

Make Waves encourages readers to step up and be the one to initiate change in their work and lives. Author Patti B. Johnson walks readers through the tools and techniques that they can use to create change in their own situations; elaborating on these tools gives readers a sense of how to encourage and instill these "wave-making" behaviors within their organization.

Using case studies as illustrative examples, *Make Waves* highlights the important steps that individuals can take toward positive change, bridging the gap between desires and actions necessary to realize bigger changes.

This new edition provides a more current and timely view of change with the expansion of the section on the mindset of a Wave Maker and more current examples.

New areas of focus are:

- How our thoughts drive our readiness to change
- Our personal "backpacks" and what we carry with us into every situation regardless of the facts, and the importance of knowing our "go-to's" and triggers
- Our habits drive almost half of our daily decisions, yet a change requires us to approach our work and life differently
- The most common obstacles to thinking like a Wave Maker

Make Waves
Be the One to Start Change at Work and in Life

Second Edition

Patti B. Johnson

Routledge
Taylor & Francis Group

A PRODUCTIVITY PRESS BOOK

First published 2025
by Routledge
605 Third Avenue, New York, NY 10158

and by Routledge
4 Park Square, Milton Park, Abingdon, Oxon, OX14 4RN

Routledge is an imprint of the Taylor & Francis Group, an informa business

© 2025 Patti B. Johnson

The right of Patti B. Johnson to be identified as author of this work has been asserted by them in accordance with sections 77 and 78 of the Copyright, Designs and Patents Act 1988.

ISBN: 978-1-032-71532-2 (hbk)
ISBN: 978-1-032-71534-6 (pbk)
ISBN: 978-1-032-71533-9 (ebk)

DOI: 10.4324/9781032715339

Typeset in Minion
by codeMantra

Dedication

To my family, who has supported me always, but especially by encouraging me to make this book a reality. You help me keep perspective and remember what really matters in life. And, you never let me forget that laughter makes everything better.

Contents

PART 1   What You Think

Acknowledgments

Love and gratitude to my husband, Jim. I could never have written the original book or the 2nd edition without him. He encouraged and supported me at every step along the way.

A very special thank you to my amazing PeopleResults friends and partners for being there and giving me so much support, interest, and wisdom throughout the years.

I appreciate Josh Getzler, my agent, for believing in this book at the beginning before it was fully formed and helping me make it a reality. Thank you to Erika Heilman and Jill Friedlander for their original commitment to "the wave" and for seeing the possibilities.

A big thank you to my people. Patrick, for being my motivator and using my own advice back on me at just the right time! Love and thanks to my son Will, who reviewed and cared. Thank you to Matt and Allison for being on my team. And thanks to my brother, Mike, for rolling up his sleeves to help and sharing so many good baseball stories.

My life has been blessed with so many friends, family, and colleagues who have given their time to offer wise counsel, make an introduction, and care when I needed it most. I am grateful to each of you.

Preface

I wrote *Make Waves* because deciding to make a change – and knowing how to do it – was behind every important goal I've ever had. I dreamed of changing the course of my career to get more control of my life and have interesting work. But starting a consulting business felt so out of reach. Yet, learning to make that change was fundamental to creating the life I wanted.

And, in my work, I couldn't escape the change word. Change was ever present with all my clients as they wanted to make their organizations and teams better and learn to work differently. Change is the constant under-current in our lives, so our only choice is to learn to thrive in this ambiguity. Sometimes, the change is a dream we designed. But, other times, it's a change that shows up on our doorstep when we didn't get a vote.

I wrote *Make Waves* to give you the tools and ideas to navigate the change in your work and in your life. We would be experts by now if all we needed was a great change model. But change depends on changing human behavior. Our behavior. So, I began researching those who had started successful changes – from entrepreneurs to college students to community champions and business leaders. I wanted to dissect how they thought, the decisions they made, and how they did it. Surprisingly, there were many common themes even across this diverse group. I added that research to my decades of experience advising clients on change and created the Wave Maker DNA – a profile of those who activate change.

We begin the exploration of change in *Make Waves* by looking at how you think about change—which determines if you'll ever start. Then, we discuss how to identify what you need to learn and understand in a very new situation. Finally, we look at essential actions and how agile planning, experimentation, and incrementalism are just a few of the difference-makers. This book is packed with practical examples, stories, insights, and wisdom from those who made their change work. I hope they will give you the inspiration and tools to go for your change.

You, too, can be a Wave Maker and start your unique path to making your change a reality – regardless of whether it's a change effort at work or in life. Taking the first step can be the hardest yet most important. In the wise words of the great Tina Fey, "You can't be that kid standing at the top of the waterslide, overthinking it. You have to go down the chute."

About the Author

Patti B. Johnson is a recognized expert on leading and starting change. She was the CEO of PeopleResults, a successful change and learning consulting firm she founded 20 years ago, and now serves as Executive Advisor. She created the original best-seller *Make Waves: Be the One to Start Change at Work and in Life* eight years ago. She was asked to update this version with new stories and expanded insights on how our thoughts drive any change.

Patti hosts the podcast *Be a Wave Maker: Conversations on Change*, and she is on the Board of Directors at Pariveda Solutions.

Patti and her team have advised clients such as PepsiCo, McKesson, Microsoft, 7-Eleven, Frito-Lay, JLL, Honeywell, and many others on creating positive change in their leaders and organizations. She has advised many leaders on leading large organizational transformations and on the individual behaviors that make a real difference.

Previously, Patti was a senior executive at Accenture and held numerous global leadership positions while specializing in client projects with complex people transitions. She was also the strategic leader for global People & Talent.

Patti is Adjunct Faculty for the SMU Cox School of Business. She has been featured in the *Harvard Business Review, The Wall Street Journal, The New York Times, Fast Company, MONEY Magazine, U.S. News and World Report, Fortune*, and many more.

1

What's Your Wave?

THINK.KNOW.DO

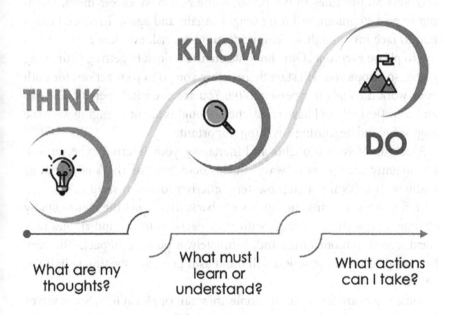

Almost everyone wants to make a change in their lives: change careers, get healthier, connect or help others, redesign how their team works, or start a new business. These changes range from small ideas that affect only you to big ideas with far-reaching impact.

DOI: 10.4324/9781032715339-1

The purpose of this book is to encourage you to believe that creating positive change isn't as hard as you may think.

There are many great change models and frameworks. Yet, I've come to believe that successful changes ultimately come down to our thoughts and behaviors. If models got us there—we'd be pros at change. The hardest part is both being willing to dream and then taking the first step. This book is designed for you to help you move your dream change forward.

When I think about my goals and changes in my life, the number one barrier for me was my thoughts. I doubted myself, was hard on myself, and wanted everything to be great—when there were times it just couldn't be for me or for everyone else. But yet, my thoughts were also the original domino that got me to advance in my career, start a business, write a book, and eventually lead our business acquisition. I have faced the same thoughts and hurdles in my personal life as a busy career mom, learning to be a stepmom, or losing weight. Again and again, I realized that I had to face my thoughts—fear, perfectionism, risk avoidance, and wanting to please everyone. Our thoughts are the unlock to getting your thing going, so I hope you will start there before you go to your actions for both your work life and your personal life. You are one whole person. For me, and countless others I have researched, thoughts about changing were the engine behind beginning anything important.

Speaking of your thoughts and managing your internal expectations, I frequently use the term "wave" in this book because that's how change really works. It's not a step-by-step, orderly process; instead, it's messy, with five steps forward and three steps back. That's just the nature of any change. But, a change begins with your decision to act and ripples outward, creating momentum and, ultimately, a positive impact. The very first small decision or action will build as it goes. So, starting is half the battle!

Some waves are far-reaching. Some are small ripples at first. Some waves happen inside a family or an organization, while others sweep over a community or market. The common denominator is that one person saw a need or opportunity and decided to be the one to start a change.

And waves don't have to begin with those who have the most important title or the greatest experience. As this book highlights, the new professional, the first-time entrepreneur, the student, or the leader in a Fortune 500 company can all start a change.

FINDING YOUR WAVE

What change is waiting for you? When you take time to dream, how do you finish the sentence, "If only..."? Finding your wave is essential for creating meaning in your work, building an impactful career, and turning your dreams into reality.

Waves are as unique as you are. You have something special to contribute. Whether your wave is big or small, this book is for you. We all have waves within us.

> **The work reveals itself as you go.**
>
> —Rick Rubin,
> *The Creative Act: A Way of Being*[1]

A VERY PERSONAL WAVE MAKER

Before diving in, let me share my perspective on making waves, which changed after a personal and very sad experience. It was a turning point when I saw this book through a different lens. You see, for many years, my family had an up-close look at someone who made waves—even though I didn't fully recognize it at the time. And even though she is gone, her ripple effects continue.

A few years ago, I received an urgent call from my husband, Jim. His mother, the matriarch of the family, had just had a massive heart attack. I knew from Jim's voice that time was running out. Helen Johnson was a force of nature; full of ideas and plans, she was the center of the family. We looked at each other sadly on that hot summer evening, wondering what we'd do without her.

More family arrived, and we sat around Helen's huge oak dining table, as we had done for so many Sunday lunches and holidays in the past. We began to do what all families do at such times: we shared stories about her life and heard many new ones from friends and neighbors who came by to remember her too.

As a young girl, Helen had worked two and three jobs to put herself through college, and her siblings pooled their savings to ensure they could all reach this goal, too. She found her life's work as a sixth-grade teacher. She helped hundreds of children who needed guidance in the classroom and an adult who cared about them and shared supplies, encouragement, and support.

She and her husband, Ed, were heartbroken when he was diagnosed with Alzheimer's upon his retirement. But Helen soon became an Alzheimer's support group leader, and she bolstered countless others when their loved ones received this devastating diagnosis. In her darkest hour, she decided to help others.

Despite her disappointments, Helen never lost her zest and love of life. She started a seniors group in her church, continued taking college classes and sharing what she learned with others, and got on social media to be where her kids and grandkids were. She was always excitedly planning the next destination for her family or girlfriends, was the first to organize a get-together to honor a friend, and was there for family members when they needed her most.

As we shared stories about Helen's decisions and actions, which didn't seem that significant when she made them, we realized that her ripple effects were astounding. Her decisions to take action and help in so many situations started cumulative changes that went well beyond what she even knew.

Her ripples started with some very simple questions. In every situation, she asked herself, "What can I do?" and "How can I help?" Then, the hard part—she did it. Her habit of accountability and her bias for action are powerful lessons in how just one person can start important changes. Her actions led to significant changes not just in the groups she was part of but in the lives of others, encouraging and lifting them up when they needed it most. My thoughts over that week of facing Helen's death helped me internalize that anyone can make a wave, and what may seem very small can be very far-reaching.

After the services, I dedicated myself to researching and studying those who have made waves. I asked trusted colleagues, "Who do you know that is a Wave Maker?" I also wanted to include people like Helen, who were ordinary people around us who made a significant impact.

Many animatedly told me about people who had inspired them by starting big or small changes. I eagerly anticipated the interviews because
of my colleagues' enthusiasm in recommending their Wave Makers.
They did not disappoint. I was riveted by stories of how these individuals began and sustained their big and small changes. Their stories are
sprinkled throughout this book as well as my own. I hope these examples and stories will be as instructional and inspire you to make your
own waves.

WAVES BEGIN WITH "IF ONLY WE COULD..."

Let me give you some examples of how one person's actions started a wave,
big or small. They all began with "If only we could..."

- The college student who organized a way to share wasted campus
  food with the homeless
- The female manager who lobbied for commitment and funding to
  start a networking group that connects younger female professionals
  to senior mentors
- The young engineering professional with an idea for a process change
  that no one had considered, yet it improved both efficiency and customer service
- The company vice president who translated her growth strategy into
  simple and clear outcomes, engaging more than three thousand
  employees to make the vision a reality
- The math teacher who convinced the school district to introduce
  a more advanced math curriculum to better prepare students for
  college

These are diverse examples, and the planning and execution of each wave
were different because of its varying scale and complexity. Yet, many common themes exist in how the individuals who started these changes think,
act, and engage with others. We'll learn from each of them as well as many
others.

LEARNING ABOUT WAVES

Make Waves is also based on the belief that we can all learn from one another's waves. I believe that a university professor's innovative way of creating a learning community is relevant for the business professional; that a student-led community event has relevance outside a college setting; that changing your habits for healthier living applies to behavioral changes at work; and that an entrepreneur's successful start-up holds valuable insights for Fortune 500 leaders. Even though each change is very different, common patterns, habits, and strategies fuel those who start any change. Together, we'll explore how your thoughts and habits can adapt to start your change and move forward.

Think, too, about the Wave Makers you already know. Who have you watched start a change? What were their very first steps? How did they react when their wave hit a wall? Adding your observations and experiences to the stories in *Make Waves* will bring you new insights, and you'll see that successful waves are happening around you.

Make Waves is designed to give you the confidence and tools to get started and challenge some of your long-held assumptions. In my work advising leaders about organizational and behavioral change, I see so much conventional wisdom that needs to be revisited. We'll question our beliefs on each long-cherished way of doing things.

We'll also look at how Wave Makers realized their goals despite some setbacks and bumps along the way. We'll learn how to assess your setbacks and develop your Plan B.

WAVE CONDITIONS

As you consider your ideas, let's look at the ingredients that make a successful wave. Waves have three key criteria:

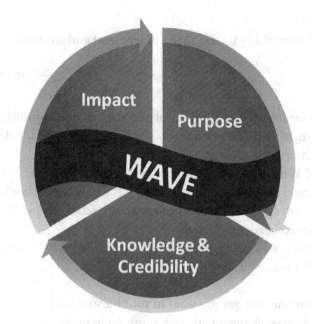

1. **A wave creates an undeniable *impact* at the right time.** A wave aims to improve your life, organization, community, or market. And the "right time" means that an idea is shared when conditions make it possible to succeed—even with resistance. Timing impacts how much attention your change receives, the pace of progress, and readiness for your ideas.

2. **A wave has a bigger *purpose*.** A wave, by design, has ripple effects. It can move forward by way of other people without you guiding every step. This progress is possible because it has meaning and purpose. We'll learn more in the coming chapters about the power of a circle and team to support you. This advocacy of an idea only happens if it has a greater purpose and value that makes a difference.

3. **A wave is built upon *knowledge* and *credibility*.** Waves require both passion and substance. You have to know your topic and understand the facts. You can get smarter yourself or invite the right experts to be your partners. You'll need knowledge, expertise, and credibility to be the champion for others. Credibility is essential in encouraging others to believe in the cause.

We tied everything we did to the bigger goal and strategy.

—Fiona Grant

Waves are meaningful and impactful and start from a knowledge source that gives them credibility. But waves start because one person decided. It begins with you.

What if? What if we changed how we grow the business? What if my business could reach customers globally? What if high school students had the knowledge and resources to earn more scholarships? What if my team felt appreciated and valued?

What if? You are the one to answer this question.

I hope that *Make Waves* will inspire you to:

- Explore the changes you want in your life and work
- Decide what changes you are committed to make
- Understand the importance of your thoughts in getting started and staying motivated
- Determine what you need to learn and better understand
- Decide the first steps you'll take to get started
- Know the habits that you need to manage or that may get in your way
- Incorporate new practices, habits, and strategies for starting a change

I wrote this book to encourage you to reflect, learn, and begin making your own waves! You'll notice questions to consider as you think about your change. I avoid using the word "steps" whenever possible because changes aren't sequential. Waves flow, growing and evolving as they move forward. Think of this book as a blueprint to give you the confidence and knowledge to get started and realize your goals.

It can be you. What's your wave?

THINK TIME

As you read, think about your wave. Here are some questions to consider:

- What changes do you want in your life and work?
- How would you describe your ideal future?
- What would improve your team, organization, or community?
- What are your passions and interests? How can you use them for a bigger purpose?
- If you could change one thing in your life, what would it be?

I encourage you to consider these questions first so that as you dive into *Make Waves*, you have your wave(s) in mind.

NOTE

1 Rick Rubin, *The Creative Act: A Way of Being* (New York; Penguin Press, 2023), p. 147.

Part 1

What You Think

2

Think Like a Wave Maker

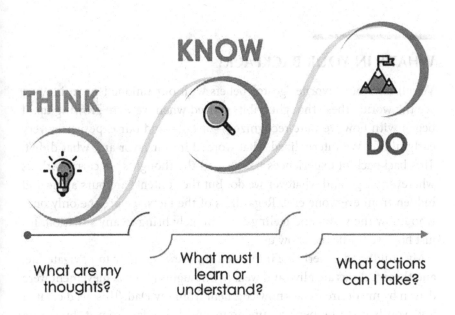

THINK.KNOW.DO

THINK — What are my thoughts?

KNOW — What must I learn or understand?

DO — What actions can I take?

We know now that any change really starts with our thoughts. Thinking is the key to everything—how you feel and your actions. Thoughts are the driver in what happens in your life and it may be the only thing you fully control. Your thoughts will determine if your wave is created and ever acted upon.

DOI: 10.4324/9781032715339-3

13

It's crazy, but this chapter wasn't even in my outline when I began writing this book. However, after I interviewed dozens of Wave Makers and really reflected on my own experiences in how individuals start successful change, it became so clear that success wasn't fueled just because of actions. How we *think* about the change will determine both if we see the change and what we decide to do about it.

In my research and experiences with clients, there are countless stories from those who began successful changes and I consistently noted their optimism, persistence, willingness to fail, and adaptability in reaching their goals. Their thoughts powered them from the very beginning and kept them moving forward.

Let's begin by exploring your favorite thoughts you always carry with you.

WHAT'S IN YOUR BACKPACK?

We all have our favorite "go-to" beliefs with our unique lens in how we see the world. These thought habits started when we were growing up. It began with how we were recognized—or not—and our experiences very early in life. We internalized what worked in our favor and what didn't. This backpack of experiences has shaped the thoughts we carry with us wherever we go and whatever we do. But the contents are ours alone and hidden from everyone else. Regardless of the facts, we are the only ones who know the views and feelings we uniquely bring to any situation. It's just how we think and show up.

My childhood experience imprinted my views on how to navigate life, and these feelings are alive and well. My thoughts about achievement were driven by my desire for acknowledgment from my Dad. This need created my "you have to be perfect" undercurrent. I was far from it, but those thoughts were always there, driving my decisions and being hard on myself when I wasn't good enough. These feelings also made me really struggle when I came up short. Likewise, as a young woman in a male-dominated business world, I learned to adapt and disguise myself to be who I needed to be. I was frequently the only woman in the leadership meeting, so I held back a bit of myself to be correct, fit in, and not screw up. My confidence grew over time as I grew and business culture began to change, but these early experiences shaped my career and comfort with transparency and vulnerability.

I'm a fan of Brené Brown and her research, including the classic, best-selling book *Daring Greatly*, which shares an insightful view of the transformational impact of vulnerability. Brown believes vulnerability is the path to conquering our fears and creating a real connection with others. These are two critical elements in starting and sustaining any wave.

Brown asserts that one of the underlying reasons for the fear of vulnerability is our scarcity culture—there is never enough to go around. We embody the scarcity culture by comparing ourselves with others, believing our change isn't significant enough, or thinking that if others have a special quality, we don't. Goodness must be in limited supply!

In her research, Brown asked people to fill in the blank: I'm *never* _____ *enough*. Some of the responses were:

- Never good enough.
- Never perfect enough.
- Never powerful enough.
- Never successful enough.
- Never smart enough.
- Never certain enough.
- Never safe enough.
- Never extraordinary enough.[1]

What is your answer? The answer to this question will likely lead you to the fears that will be the internal obstacles in starting your wave. If you never feel good enough, you are probably overly dependent upon external validation for your confidence. Your thoughts are driven by outside-in rather than inside-out.

If you never feel successful enough—you may work too much and always look to the next thing rather than maximizing today. Because you are driven by the thought of "I need to be better—this isn't quite good enough."

I also encourage you to consider your favorite thoughts regardless of the situation or the facts. These are common thoughts I've seen in working with clients:

- *I can't be wrong—or it will affect my career.*
- *I can't speak up here—or I'll be viewed negatively.*

- *I'm afraid to take a risk—so I'll hang back and see what others do.*
- *I have to be right—I'm the expert!*
- *No one supported my idea or me—it didn't work.*

These favorite thoughts imprinted in our brains create automatic habits in us. No decision is required. We are on autopilot.

What's in your backpack?

POWER OF HABITS

Our brain loves habits. Habits are designed to shortcut decision-making and drive efficiency—which is just what our brains want. Some habits work to our benefit, but others can become invisible and powerful roadblocks when we want to start or create change.

Helpful habits include:

- Brushing your teeth every day
- Working out every morning
- Starting your workday with 30 minutes of open time to purposely plan your day
- Drawing boundaries for when your workday ends unless there is a crisis
- Having story time with the kids every night before bed
- Daily meditation or prayer

Habits that can get in our way:

- Overanalyzing until you know you have the perfect answer
- Wanting to always be right, so you don't listen to or embrace new information that may change the "right answer"
- Saying yes to every incoming request so you are always behind, miss deadlines, can't honor commitments, and are exhausted
- Overvaluing complete agreement with everyone so you avoid raising problems or providing better alternatives
- Avoiding problems in hopes they will go away and you won't have to face them

Habits are ingrained in us because our brains are prediction machines. We've taught our brains what to do throughout our lives and work. Our brains love predictability and situations when we know what will happen next. The brain's primary goal is to conserve energy. The less time we have to think about a decision or process new information, the less energy our brain wastes on it. This desire for energy conservation is why our brains rely on habits for shortcuts. With no extra energy, we know what to do next without ever thinking about it. Yet, we still use these same familiar habits when they no longer serve us.

In *Atomic Habits*, an excellent book for learning to start behavior change, James Clear shares how habits are simply solutions to recurring problems. He said, "As habits are created, the level of activity in the brain *decreases*. You learn to lock in on the cues that predict success and tune out everything else. When a similar situation arises in the future, you know exactly what to look for. There is no longer a need to analyze every angle of a situation. Your brain skips the process of trial and error and creates a mental rule: if then, then that. These cognitive scripts can be followed automatically whenever the situation is appropriate."[2]

This identification of patterns can be a contributor to what makes us an expert. But what if today's situation has similarities to the past—yet it's different? Do we miss new incoming information because we are following the old script in our brains? We see examples everywhere of reliance on outdated habits in our personal and professional lives that no longer fit. For example, the technical expert promoted to manager who still dives into every detailed technical issue rather than lifting up to plan the workflow of his team; the CEO that acquires an entirely different business but makes no change to managing the combined business even though they doubled in size and added new services; the Dad who still wants to control his college son's summer schedule just like when he was 12; or the professional who stays in a job she doesn't like anymore, but at least it's familiar and predictable. Habits are the underlying culprit, often driven by our deeper fears & the contents of our backpacks.

Yet, when you want to start or lead a change, these familiar habits that have served you well in other circumstances bump up against the new way. These same habits are also the force behind "But, this is how we've always done it." Know what is in your backpack of habits and fears so you are willing and ready to explore a new and different way.

> **The biggest obstacles are our self-imposed obstacles. We have to get out of our own way and recognize we can do it.**
>
> —Tory Johnson

Fears

The word fear brings to mind a scary movie, skydiving, or public speaking—which research says is still one of our greatest fears. But I am talking about a different kind of fear. This fear is hidden deep inside our backpacks. Fear can be subtle and show up in many different ways:

- Not speaking up with an idea because you might look stupid
- Never asking for needed advice or help because you won't look strong or in control
- Staying at the same company too long because the uncertainty of a new job is too scary
- Not calling attention to yourself because it's safer to blend in
- Avoiding a recommendation that you know your boss might disagree with
- Deciding not to act because your idea might not work and could hurt your reputation
- Avoiding new technology because you don't understand it
- Staying committed to a relationship that you don't want anymore because it's easier
- Not going to the event that you know will help you because you feel uncomfortable

Fear does funny things to us. It draws a big line between our beliefs about what is important versus our actions. The goal of this section is to help you acknowledge and identify your go-to fears, as it's step one in starting your change and doing things differently.

Fear also keeps us from doing what we clearly know how to do. Mike Boulanger, previously a hitting instructor for the Baltimore Orioles and the Texas Rangers, has worked with countless professional baseball players on not only how to improve their hitting but how to think about hitting. He works with players on staying focused on their actions (what's in their control) rather than anticipating the outcome, such as batting average or home runs. He believes that focusing on actions and tuning out distractions determines who makes it in the major leagues, where the pressure is intense and expectations stay high.

Boulanger said, "If you ask players if they can walk across a two-by-four board flat on the floor and be sure they won't fall off—they will quickly say, 'Yes!' Now if you ask them if they can walk across that same two-by-four board 30 feet up in the air with 35,000 screaming fans—there is a long pause. Some aren't sure. Then you add in all the thoughts in their heads— 'It's on TV,' 'What will my Dad say?' 'If I screw up, will they send me back to AAA?' and it goes on. The consistently successful hitters limit their thoughts to the bat and reacting. They tune out the rest. They trust themselves." He explained that this ability to tune out this fear often determines who makes it in Major League Baseball and who doesn't. Having raw talent and skill isn't enough.

Many of the most accomplished athletes, such as Tom Brady, Caitlin Clark, Patrick Mahomes, and Kobe Bryant, all thrived when the pressure was highest. The pressure didn't create fear and second-guessing themselves because they found a higher gear. Most of us don't have to face thousands of screaming fans as we face our fears, but we do have to manage our fears just like these professional athletes.

The first step is anticipating your "go-to" fears when you start a change so you can anticipate your triggers and plan around them in the way that fits you. I manage my fears through learning and getting more information so I can rely on facts more than my feelings. I've also realized over time that my educated gut instinct starts to kick in the more I learn about a new situation. Preparation also really helps me, even when it's short term. Preparation gives me more confidence over my fears because I've focused on what's in my control rather than what isn't.

So, how can you cut fear down to size? As Joshua Becker shares in *Things that Matter*, "Sometimes when we look at people who are accomplishing meaningful work, we think, 'Well, it comes easy for them.' I don't think that's true. I believe most—nearly all successful people had fears to overcome along the way to become who they are. If you have a role model or mentor in your life, ask her or him about it. I think you'll find that this person has had to deal with (and is probably still dealing with) fear. Almost every human being has fears and self-doubts, worries, and anxieties. Yet they face the fear. And, they find it manageable."[3]

I had fears lurking behind every big decision I've ever made. When I started PeopleResults, my fears were going strong for about three years before I finally got the courage to do it, and I still had fears years later. I had fears of, "I've never been solely responsible for selling new projects to clients—can I do it?", "What if I don't have the income I've counted on?", "I've never started a business before—will I know what to do?" and "Will this be a good experience for our team?". And the list goes on. Yet, I knew my favorite fears and started small, educated myself, and decided it was, at first, just a one-year experiment.

As Joshua Becker pointed out in *Things That Matter*, "Overcoming fear isn't about making unwise decisions. Put a safety net in position if you need to. But what I'm saying is, be self-aware and intentional while doing it. There's a difference between being held back when you're truly not ready or the timing isn't right and being held back by fear. A desire for security can be motivated by fear. Prudence can become an excuse for procrastination."[3]

As a high school student, Wave Maker Emma Scheffler started Insulin Angels to help children and their families after they were diagnosed with diabetes. When I asked Emma about her fears, she said, "My fear was, did anyone want this? Would the kids want to talk to me? At first, when I'd meet the kids at the hospital, I'd ask them to tell me their story, and then I'd tell them mine. I decided I'd rather visit the hospital and maybe not help them than not go and miss someone who really needed it."

It's also essential to recognize the fears of others when you want to include them in your change. Resistance to change often has a direct line to fear—of not knowing the answer, looking stupid, discomfort, and putting comfort above learning something new.

For example, one of our clients had resistance from field personnel to using iPads onsite with customers and recording important information. These experienced technicians previously relied on a more manual process they had used for years. And they completely understood it. After this company's significant investment in new tools and systems, they still had a very low adoption rate by their technicians. Their fear created an underlying resistance to using new technology. It was completely new, and they didn't want to feel they didn't know how to do their job. They received training but didn't ask any questions in that big forum. Instead, they relied on an all-time favorite—denial and just kept doing their work the old way. The field personnel weren't comfortable with the new technology and lacked the confidence to use it with customers. The new plan educated a core group who became learning "buddies" with the broader team so they could learn the new technology quietly and at their own pace. This education approach addressed the larger fear of working differently and gave them the space to ask questions and "not look stupid"—their biggest fear.

These technicians are not unique. We all have our favorite obstacles that get in our way.

OUR FAVORITE OBSTACLES TO STARTING A CHANGE

In my experience working with client teams and leaders, these are the three most common thought obstacles to starting a change. And the hard part is that the first two are often attributes that have propelled our success.

1. **Perfectionism**

What do perfectionists want most of all? To be perfect, have it right and be recognized for it! If that is your ultimate goal—you'll likely stay in one place too long. You think you need a little more information, analysis, or input before you decide. Otherwise, how can you be sure your plan is perfect?

Yet, perfectionism is often worn as a badge of honor. When the job interviewer asks you about your areas for development, candidates will say, "I'm a perfectionist!" It's right up there with "I work too much." It is a trait that many are proud to claim and share as a positive.

Let's also be honest. Many of us, myself included, have examples of when our perfectionist tendencies are what made the presentation great or the client project a big success. Perfectionism includes being fully prepared—which always helps. I frequently lead *Leading Change* workshops and I know every variation of the content cold— yet I always make sure I'm fully prepared, run through the slides, and practice. I don't want to jinx myself or feel I'm not taking the workshop seriously. But, at heart, I think it's perfectionism at play.

Let's compare perfectionist tendencies and how they fit with the realities of any change. Any change is new—probably not something you've done before; there will be surprises. Any change evolves and takes shape as you go. You don't have the luxury of sitting back until all facts are known because everything is moving too fast. Perfectionists feel tension because, despite the need to move faster, the risk of failure is too great. So, they slow down decisions or even procrastinate in their quest for perfection. Research even shows a direct correlation between perfectionism and procrastination. If you want everything perfect, any decision might not lead to the perfect outcome. So, maybe it's better to wait.

In a change, if you have all the answers—you've waited too long.

Tammie Pinkston,
executive change consultant

In *Four Thousand Weeks: Time Management for Mortals*, Oliver Burkeman argues that this type of "procrastination means we are more comfortable with an idealized fantasy of what could be rather than the limitations and unpredictability of reality." He said, "We fail to see, or refuse to accept, that any attempt to bring our ideas into concrete reality must inevitably fall short of our dreams, no matter how brilliantly we succeed in carrying things off—because reality, unlike fantasy, is a realm in which we don't have limitless control, and can't possibly hope to meet our perfectionist standards... Dispiriting as this may sound at first...if you're procrastinating on something because you're worried you won't do a good enough job, you can relax—because judged by the flawless standards of your imagination, you definitely *won't* do a good enough job. So, you might as well make a start."[4]

The Expert

The Expert's brand is being right, having the answers, and the one who always knows. This brand is intertwined with the work of some professions. For example, attorneys, doctors, CPAs, or the main contact for benefit questions are expected to always know the right answer. In a change, it's not just about technical knowledge but how you size up the situation—the overall change.

The Expert is very uncomfortable with not knowing all the answers. They feel vulnerable and exposed without the protection of their knowledge and experience. The most common obstacles I see for the Expert in times of high change are:

— Applying yesterday's successful answers to today's new problems
— Ignoring new information because they aren't the obvious expert anymore if they acknowledge conditions have changed
— Having blindspots on what will be needed in the change
— Not listening enough as they want to be the one who already knows.

The expert phenomenon can be even more pronounced with senior executives and those with the most experience. Their knowledge got them here, and their title may be their ace. But, in the wise words of Marshall Goldsmith, "What got you here won't get you there."

2. **Being Very, Very Comfortable**

To be clear, this obstacle isn't laziness or lack of effort. But instead, someone who values predictability and routine above everything. This thought obstacle causes us to stay in jobs or relationships we no longer want to be in or ignore what we want most in life—because a predictable routine matters more than anything else. There is a connection between what we have in our backpacks and the reliance on routine.

If you put routine and predictability first—you likely most value security, safety, and feeling comfortable. The desire to always know and control what happens next takes the wheel and causes you to avoid new information, see a better way, and even make decisions that aren't in your best interest.

As I mentioned, when I started PeopleResults, I had some big fears. I had a great career and knew I could carry on in leadership roles in large organizations. I was comfortable and understood how that model worked. Yet, I wanted my unique blend of career growth and control of my life, especially when the boys were younger. But making the jump to being an entrepreneur with no predictable income or support? My desire for predictability (along with a hefty dose of perfectionism) slowed me down. It took me almost three years to build up the courage to step out and start a business. But I used that time to educate myself and talk to dozens of people who knew a lot about creating a successful business. This education made a huge difference for me. Even then, I "tricked" myself into thinking of this new venture as an experiment that I would assess at the end of one year to determine if it was right for me. I am not as bold as some entrepreneurs, but I met myself where I was and found my way to take the first step. This mindset worked for me as I began picturing a different career.

See the Unseen

Wave Makers set aside their fears to see the unseen opportunity. They can see what isn't in front of them today. They know their "why" and aren't limited by today or stuck in the status quo. They are open to "what if?" and are committed to reaching their goals. These practical dreamers believe in what they can envision, even when others can't.

> **Follow your own internal thermostat more than the external thermostat.**
>
> —**Clint Hurdle**

Those who start changes are much more motivated by their change's impact or purpose than by a desire for personal recognition. The Wave Makers I've known are passionate about their cause—from promoting good health to improving patient care to building a different kind of business. While they certainly saw risks and had fears, they didn't let their concerns prevent them from taking action. They were motivated by the belief that the change would improve their organization, group, or client experience. They were committed to moving forward and making progress through being passionate, informed, and persistent.

Allen Stephenson, Wave Maker and creator of Southern Tide, an American apparel company, shared his motivation from the beginning of his career when he was 22. Asked if he had any fears when he started, Allen answered:

"I really didn't. But I also knew that I had to put everything into it. That meant I had to give up my social life and all my hobbies. I quit school. I had no money because I spent it all on the business. I moved back into my parents' house. I didn't buy anything, and I worked about fifteen to sixteen hours a day, every day, for a couple of years. I knew I could do it; it was just a matter of if I would be dedicated enough. I knew that I would, because, heck, I dropped out of college. So if I screwed up, I wouldn't have had anything to fall back on. And almost everybody thought it wouldn't work, except for my mom. Almost everyone else thought I was crazy. I don't really care if people think I'm crazy. But the deck was stacked against me in every possible way if I didn't succeed—financially, educationally, socially. I had to do it."

I found that those who start and sustain successful changes have a particular way of thinking. Wave Makers typically:

- Acknowledge and manage their fears
- See possibilities
- See the opportunity while understanding the risk
- Ask, "What can I do?"
- Know what they don't know
- Picture themselves as who they *want* to be, not who they are today

You may think that some people are just naturally creative or innovative and others aren't, but that isn't true, according to researchers Jeff Dyer and Hal Gregersen in their book *Innovator's DNA: Mastering the Five Skills of Disrupting Innovators*. "You learn to see what isn't there today by habitually asking the right questions: 'Why?' 'Why must it be that way?' 'What if?' 'What's the alternative?'"

Let's look at Steve Jobs as the gold standard for seeing the unseen. Dyer and Gregersen note, "So what do we learn from Jobs's ability to think different? Well, first, we see that his innovative ideas didn't spring fully formed from his head, as if they were a gift from the Idea Fairy. When we examine the origins of these ideas, we typically find that the catalyst was:

- a question that challenged the status quo
- an observation of a technology, company, or customer
- an experience or experiment where he was trying out something new
- a conversation with someone who alerted him to an important piece of knowledge or opportunity."[5]

This natural curiosity and openness to new information began the formation of new ideas. I found that most Wave Makers relied on this curiosity and exploration in approaching opportunities and addressing problems.

Reframing Thoughts to Action

We've discussed addressing your habits & fears first and then finding the path to move forward. For example, if your obstacle is fear of making a mistake or risk avoidance, look for a small, low-risk action as your first step. Or, if you have a bias for wanting approval, internally anchor to your "why" so that you can rely on your purpose rather than overplaying resistance. Identify the thoughts that will get you comfortable with taking action.

As Rich Sheridan, CEO of Menlo Innovations, shared, "I realized that the first thing I had to change was me. I had to start thinking differently. I had to see the world differently than everybody else. I came to accept that different was more than okay."

Ask, "What Can I Do Now?"

Asking yourself this question is the simplest way to move from thoughts into action and progress. There is always an answer. In high-stress, confusing situations, the "now" might be just a small step today because that is as far as you can see.

If you believe you can contribute, make a difference, and start a change— you start by asking yourself how you can start and take the first small step.

Wave Maker Guwan Jones, former leader of Diversity and Inclusion at Baylor Scott & White, helped her leadership translate their commitment to diversity into a direct impact on the quality of patient care. She said, "There's always a cause and effect. I feel strongly that patients who aren't experiencing some likeness to their cultural background and to those things that are important to them are much less likely to pay attention to the advice we give them. And, when there are too many of the same, like-minded people in a room making decisions about patient care, it's not beneficial for patients. It makes us better when we have more than one opinion."

Guwan kept the bigger purpose in mind as she approached her change. When I asked her what made her take on this wave, she said: "It was that I could put together diversity and workforce analytics and impact the quality of patient care. And that hadn't really been done before. I wanted to figure out how to get it done. I kept hearing over and over from people that 'You're just so transparent.' And so, I guess that has given me the latitude to ask questions and delve into things because I am very open. I'll share exactly what's on my mind and what I'm thinking. You know, I'm very honest. It may work out; it may not work out. But I really think there's something there and this is what I'd like to do. And, I've been given opportunities to just do that—to go find it and make it work."

She started with "What can I do?" and "How can I make a difference?" This question helped her move from idea to action.

Wave Makers don't wait for others to act or assume someone else will take on the change. Some Wave Makers see opportunities or know the business needs to solve a problem. Others start a change because the opportunity is right there in front of them, and they know they have to take it. Many take a relatively small first step without realizing that a larger wave will follow. You'll remember my stories about Helen Johnson, my mother-in-law, and the ripples she created in her life that all began with seemingly small decisions.

Wave Maker Joe Nussbaum started The Big Event at Texas A&M, the largest one-day, student-run service project in the nation, and the concept has expanded to 75 other schools. Nussbaum said, "I thought we should do some things to encourage more student service work. The President had started a big initiative about volunteerism. It made us think, 'What can we do?'"

Joe said he woke up one night, and it was clear what needed to be done. He explained, "We came up with the idea to have a large, coordinated effort to match up student groups with community organizations to create this huge service project on the same day. It started when we put together the request for volunteerism with what we could do at A&M."

Like the change led by Joe and his fellow students, waves start when a person ready to take the first step asks, "What can I do?" and "How can I make a difference?"

THE DNA OF WAVE MAKERS

In my research on those who start changes, I saw patterns not just in how they think or what they do, but in the way they approach life and work. I didn't want to miss this in Make Waves. I don't see the Wave Makers and others I interviewed as superhuman, but I saw in them particular behaviors and beliefs that make up who they are; these patterns help them when starting a wave, doing their work, or being a trusted family member or a friend.

I've outlined the four key elements of Wave Maker DNA that lay the foundation for the way they approach their lives and work overall—beyond a wave or change.

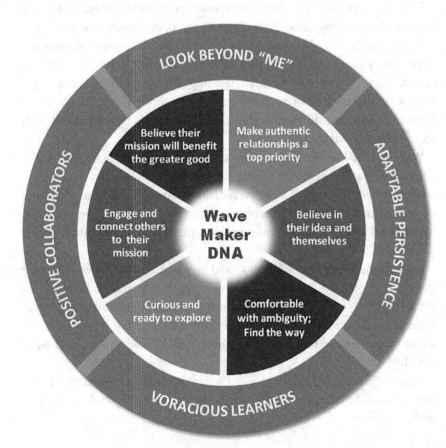

LOOK BEYOND "ME"

Wave Makers place more importance on reaching the goal than on personal recognition. They are driven by the anticipated impact and change rather than personal accolades. This approach keeps them motivated even when setbacks or detours occur. In addition, they:

- Believe their mission will benefit the greater good. Wave Makers create momentum around an idea that reaches beyond self to make work, the community, or the world better. They are more focused on "what's in it for us" than "what's in it for me."
- Make authentic relationships a top priority. Wave Makers place a high priority on the meaningful and diverse relationships needed to achieve their goals. They are interested in being helpful to others. Relationships help them learn, build a strong network, and find meaning in their work.

ADAPTABLE PERSISTENCE

Wave Makers have a healthy balance of persistence toward a goal while also adapting and adjusting when they get new information. Not deterred by setbacks, they are open to new ideas and insights. Wave Makers don't give up on the goal but remain flexible on how it is accomplished. They also:

- Believe in their idea and themselves. Wave Makers believe in their ability to reach their goals in spite of obstacles. Grounded in their mission, they are both passionate about their idea and resourceful. They have a healthy confidence in realizing the goal without getting distracted or mired in future details.

VORACIOUS LEARNERS

Wave Makers are always looking to enhance their knowledge and insights. Wave Makers seek out experts, read, listen, and build mentoring relationships. They are comfortable taking on a new idea or topic because they have confidence that they can learn what they need to know. Wave Makers:

- Are comfortable with ambiguity; they find the way. Guided by a strong belief in themselves and their goal, they have a bias for action and can move forward with a plan that has unknowns. They know when and how to seek expert advice for new insights as they move forward.
- Are curious and ready to explore. Wave Makers often ask, "Why?" and "What if?" It's in their nature to want to understand, apply new ideas to their work, and explore. Wave Makers examine topics that, on the surface, may not seem linked to their work, but they see connections.

POSITIVE COLLABORATORS

Wave Makers generally start from an intention of positivity and trust. They have a bias for transparency and authenticity in how they work with others. They aren't driven by ego as much as by a desire to work together toward a shared goal. In addition, they:

- Engage and connect others to the mission. Wave Makers know that the way they communicate with others is vital to advancing their idea. They know that it is important to share their goals with many people to ensure their idea's survival. They translate the meaning and purpose through stories that are relevant and meaningful to others.

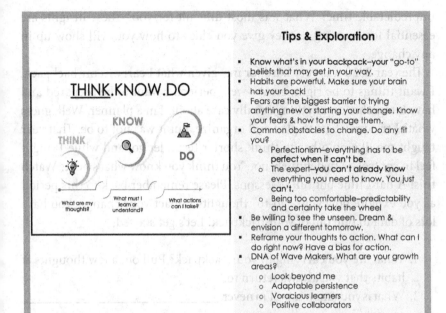

THINK.KNOW.DO

KNOW

THINK

DO

What are my thoughts?

What must I learn or understand?

What actions can I take?

Tips & Exploration

- Know what's in your backpack—your "go-to" beliefs that may get in your way.
- Habits are powerful. Make sure your brain has your back!
- Fears are the biggest barrier to trying anything new or starting your change. Know your fears & how to manage them.
- Common obstacles to change. Do any fit you?
  o Perfectionism—everything has to be perfect when it can't be.
  o The expert—you can't already know everything you need to know. You just can't.
  o Being too comfortable—predictability and certainty take the wheel
- Be willing to see the unseen. Dream & envision a different tomorrow.
- Reframe your thoughts to action. What can I do right now? Have a bias for action.
- DNA of Wave Makers. What are your growth areas?
  o Look beyond me
  o Adaptable persistence
  o Voracious learners
  o Positive collaborators

THINK TIME

Before you dive into Think Time, let's explore your reactions to a prior change. In March 2020, we all experienced COVID-19 as one of our lifetime's most significant, immediate, and collective changes we all experienced together. COVID changed almost everything in our lives. In the past, when I led change workshops, we'd often discuss a case study to explore a common hypothetical change together. But 2020 and COVID created the universal case study for how we adapt to and manage through unplanned change.

That year I made decisions in the morning that were completely obsolete by that night. At that time, our line of sight for decisions was a few days at best. The pandemic changed how we worked and interacted with friends and family—well, just about everything. How did it affect your thoughts and feelings? What helped you cope during this tumultuous and unpredictable time? What was most difficult for you? These insights are essential for learning as they give you clues to how you will show up in any change.

The year 2020 was very hard for me, given what I carry in my backpack. I want things to be right, great—well, perfect. I want to be prepared and have it together on anything I really care about. I'm a planner. Well, guess what? I tried my best to plan and organize, but it was not to be. That year taught me like no other to think shorter term, let go, and while I might feel in control—I'm definitely not. You think you know what's next? Watch this! A hard time but full of lessons. Please remember back to this period as you explore how your "go-to" thoughts impact your change. You have lots of data to pull out of your backpack! Let's get started.

1. What are you carrying in your backpack? Pull out a few thoughts & habits that you always return to.
2. What is your answer to "I'm never _____ enough"?
3. What are your most common go-to fears?
4. What worked in your favor during COVID? What worked against you?
5. What did you learn about your adaptability to change during COVID?
6. What caused you to have these fears?
7. How will these fears affect your ability to start your change?
8. How would you describe your risk tolerance?
9. In what situations are you most comfortable? What situations create the most fear or discomfort?
10. What strategies have worked for you in the past in moving past fear?
11. What is your "why" for taking on this change?
12. What goals do you have for changing your thinking so you see the need and can act upon it?

NOTES

1 Brené Brown, *Daring Greatly* (New York: Gotham, 2012), pp. 24–25.
2 James Clear, *Atomic Habits* (New York: Penguin Random House, 2018), p. 45.

3 Joshua Becker, *Things That Matter* (Colorado Springs, CO: Waterbrook, imprint of Penguin Random House LLC, 2022), pp. 46, 49.
4 Oliver Burkeman, *Four Thousand Weeks* (New York: Farrar, Straus and Giroux, 2021), pp. 79–80.
5 Clayton M. Christensen, Jeff Dyer, and Hal Gregersen, *Innovator's DNA: Mastering the Five Skills of Disrupting Innovators* (Boston: Harvard Business Press, 2011), p. 21.

Part 2

What You Know

3

What You Need to Know

THINK.<u>KNOW</u>.DO

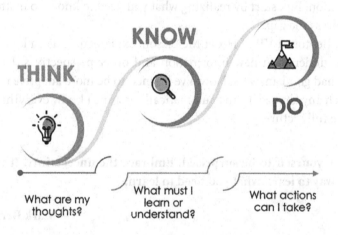

THINK — What are my thoughts?

KNOW — What must I learn or understand?

DO — What actions can I take?

You are about to embark on something new. A change you haven't done before. A new experience! Recognizing this means you can't already know everything you need to know or have all the answers.

In my experiences with Wave Makers, I'm always amazed that at the very beginning, they often knew absolutely nothing about their eventual wave. Picture the software entrepreneur who knew nothing about starting a new business before she began, the apparel company creator who had never designed a shirt before and knew nothing about apparel production, the leader who had never created a program for a global audience, or the high school student who knew absolutely nothing about non-profits. Yet, none stopped at the thought, "I don't know how to do this." Instead,

DOI: 10.4324/9781032715339-5

they thought, "I can learn this," "I can figure this out," and "I will find the right experts on whatever I can't learn." They understood the knowledge gap and set about closing it. They offer two key insights for us: (1) they acknowledged they didn't already know everything they needed to know, and (2) they didn't stop their dream because of it either.

In Chapter 2, we discussed how our need to be the expert and already have the answers gets in our way. In any change, it's essential to ask yourself, "What do I need to learn to do this well?" There is always an answer. This question starts with awareness and ends with a plan to get smarter on closing your gap because you will have one.

Also, decide if you need experts to help you know what to do. You may not be able to learn everything you need to know in the timeframe you need to know it. Rely on others to close your gap. Use AI to gather more information. But, start by realizing what you need to know no matter how you address the gap.

Mark Benton, a VP of HR at McKesson, explained, "I ask a lot of questions to understand new information and other perspectives. I used to think I had good answers. Now, I've learned to be more adaptive in how I approach any change. I can't automatically assume I know everything and have the full picture."

> Allow yourself to be surprised. Embrace the uncertainty. It's the best way to learn what you need to learn.
>
> —Mark Benton

CRITICAL MINDSET & BEHAVIORS

As a backdrop, let's consider the mindset and behaviors that fuel knowing what you need to know and acting on it.

Curiosity

Research says that, statistically, curiosity peaks at about age four and then declines through adulthood. We become too busy, feel we should already know, and lose our wonderment of the world around us. Yet, curiosity is at the root of learning, creativity, and innovation.

As Leon Seltzer, Ph.D., author of Evolution of Self, points out in a *Psychology Today* article, "Curiosity is Invaluable", "That's why many authors have argued that curiosity makes us more intelligent—enhancing our critical thinking skills and making us more likely to question assumptions, challenge beliefs, assess evidence, and so make better, more informed decisions. Albert Einstein stated that 'curiosity is more important than intelligence'. Moreover, curiosity intensifies our imagination and sparks creativity, prompting us to think outside the box and generate new ideas."[1]

If any of you have a four or five-year-old child, grandchild, niece, or nephew, you know their favorite question. "Why?" "Why can't dogs talk?" or "Why can some people run faster than other people?" The list goes on. They embrace curiosity. Of course, we can't go through life asking questions all day and still get anything done or have anyone want to talk with us! Yet, that sense of curiosity and wonder is at the core of learning and exploration.

Listening

A key ingredient of learning and curiosity is listening. Listening is critical in any change effort for two key reasons: (1) it is one of the primary ways you gain new information from others and (2) it is essential for building trust and connection. There is nothing we love more than feeling heard. Listening enables shared goals and good relationships. All critical in any wave.

I think listening skills are the most underutilized superpower in business. If I ask my clients what gets in the way of better listening skills, the number one answer is not having enough time and being in a hurry. You think listening will slow you down, yet you'll miss critical information if you don't listen. And listening has taken a backseat to sharing. In our social world, there is much more emphasis on what *we* want to say and put out into the world. Will others follow me? Will they like my content?

In the classic business and leadership book, *7 Habits of Highly Effective People*, legendary author Stephen Covey shares, "Most people do not listen with the intent to understand; they listen with the intent to reply."[2] I love this quote because it is so true. We want to show we already know the answer! We are smart! Wait until you hear what I have to say! Meanwhile, no new information is coming in. We repeat what we already think or know.

For most of us, our listening skills are rusty. I encourage you to spend tomorrow asking questions and really listening. Ask follow-up questions to understand. Don't grab the conversation back and start talking about yourself. You will be amazed by the new information you'll take in with just a little effort to pause and entirely focus on the other person.

I asked the group to do a simple listening exercise in a recent client meeting. Their assignment was to ask their partner one starter question and four open-ended follow-up questions. The starter question was, "Why did you choose your career?" Simple, right? However, new information poured in on the follow-up questions as the listeners learned how many life and career decisions were made at every step, for example, the change in a college major because of a parent's opinion, the tough decision to relocate because of their partner's job opportunity, or the new career they pursued when it was risky to do so. After this 10-minute exercise, this group was amazed at all they learned about their teammates—many of whom had worked together for years. They obtained a wealth of knowledge in just 10 minutes by simply asking questions and listening—a valuable lesson for us all. Listening doesn't have to take too much time.

Picture people in your life who are great listeners. For most of us, the list isn't long. My Mom was a great listener. I thought of her because she made time to listen, asked follow-up questions, remembered prior conversations, and connected them to today. She didn't interrupt and was interested. She also asked thought-provoking questions that made me think and come to my point of view. Who are your great listeners? In a recent workshop, we discussed that great listeners are fully present. They aren't constantly glancing down at their phones—an everyday habit. In a recent interview, Simon Sinek, a life and business thought leader, said that just holding your phone—even if you aren't looking at it—signals you aren't fully engaged.

POTENTIAL OBSTACLES TO LEARNING

Conventional Wisdom

Conventional wisdom is a fancy way of saying, "This is how we do things around here." Let's explore conventional wisdom, as it can be a significant obstacle to learning a new way and taking in new information. Conventional wisdom also has roots in the status quo, commonly held beliefs not always based on fact, and simplistic headlines. Conventional wisdom is based on the past, so it runs counter to any new change. Simple beliefs such as "A woman can't be a successful CEO in this industry," "They've had this process for a long time—they'll never change," to "People will never pay strangers to drive them to their destination."

"Conventional wisdom" is a term used to describe beliefs generally accepted as truth. It is so strong that it is assumed to be fact—without validation. The term is often credited to the economist John Kenneth Galbraith, who used it in his 1958 book, *The Affluent Society:* "The ease with which an idea is understood + the degree to which it helps one's personal wellbeing = Conventional Wisdom."[3]

Let's deconstruct conventional wisdom. Galbraith's definition clearly states that it isn't based on facts or information. Also, consider the *ease* with which an idea is understood. If you take this phrase literally, we greatly value our ability to grasp a topic or concept easily. Some people rely on conventional wisdom while considering complex issues with hundreds of interdependencies. The matter is too complicated to understand and absorb easily, so conventional wisdom, which is already constructed, fits like a glove. It's easier that way. This is true for many political topics, business issues, and cultural differences that are complex and can't be quickly understood.

The second part of the definition concerns "the degree to which it helps one's personal well-being." So this means that if the belief benefits us personally, we are more likely to buy into it. If it fits our priorities, our agenda, or our goals, conventional wisdom can be unchallenged or not scrutinized. This bumps right up against the innate resistance to change and our affection for the status quo. The ugly side of conventional wisdom is that it can perpetuate sexism, racism, and other prejudices.

We are all working with the same conventional wisdom about how change happens in organizations, the market, and communities. If taken seriously, these pieces of "wisdom" may keep you from ever seeing the opportunity, much less getting started.

One of my favorite classic examples of conventional wisdom is in baseball. Consider Bill James's impact on baseball by introducing sabermetrics, an empirical analysis of baseball. Sabermetrics was invented in 1976 when James, an economics major and baseball fanatic, worked as a night watchman in Kansas. As a complete baseball outsider, he began to test the assumptions baseball clubs had been using for over a hundred years to see if they stood up to modern statistical analysis.

James started self-publishing his conclusions long before blogging and podcasting existed, yet his methods took hold with other baseball fans interested in statistical analysis. The movement grew entirely outside of traditional baseball—of baseball executives, scouts, broadcasters, and commentators. How could a group of people who had never played the game know anything about how baseball is really played, much less be experts?

The first major league baseball team to use sabermetrics for making player and strategy decisions was the 2002 Oakland Athletics. The story was told in the book *Moneyball* by Michael Lewis and in the movie of the same name.[4] While the movie focused on Billy Beane, the general manager, the real story began with a young person with self-acquired knowledge and the ability to see something others didn't.

General manager Billy Beane had only $40 million to spend on players, yet he had to compete against big-market teams spending $200 million. James's wave informed the thinking behind Beane's assistant GM, Paul DePodesta, a Harvard-educated sabermetrics expert who had never played the game either. Following Bill James's road map, DePodesta created a sabermetric profile that showed proven ability based on metrics, yet those in traditional baseball undervalued this information. The Oakland Athletics went on to win the American League West that year despite losing three of their best players and with the lowest player budget in the league.

Bill James started the wave that transformed baseball, though he had no authority, no official role, and had never played the game.

Wave Maker Bruce Ballengee challenged conventional wisdom when he created Pariveda Solutions. He wanted to build a company dedicated to individual growth, development, learning, and rapid advancement, not just profit. FinFest, the Pariveda Solutions internal company-wide conference, has been entirely devoted to learning and capability development, not financials or processes. Bruce changed how the organization approached selling and building client relationships and made compensation fully transparent for everyone. Bruce explained that it can be a big change when someone with a great deal of previous experience joins Pariveda Solutions because so much of the conventional wisdom associated with consulting work and organizational life has been set aside.

Lindsay Pender, a Wave Maker and nurse had 6 years of experience yet she influenced the change in neonatal ICU unit policies at her new, smaller hospital. She was the newest and youngest nurse, but she brought knowledge from the hospital where she'd previously worked, which boasted a nationally known advanced care unit. The change happened because she, like her fellow nurses, was committed to helping babies in the neonatal ICU.

It can be easy to think, "I'm not in a position to change anything. What can I do?" There are many examples of people who started their wave because they set aside the conventional wisdom that changes must start at the top or from someone with a particular title.

Not Sure I Can Do It

You can never start learning what you need to know if you can't get past thoughts of "I could never do that" or "That's too much for me to learn." These thoughts will shut you down. If it's a lack of confidence because the hill seems too high—ask yourself, "If I <u>had</u> to reach this goal or make this change, how could it be done?" You might learn more yourself or it may require another expert. You have to figure out how to close your gap.

> **Don't let your lack of knowledge get in the way. You can always find someone to help you.**
>
> —Emma Scheffler

This book is full of stories with Wave Makers, people just like you and me, who took a "I can figure it out" mindset and got going. Brooke Averick went from preschool teacher to successful podcaster and content creator after posting a few funny videos on TikTok that went viral and started her following. Allen Stephenson, founder of Southern Tide, immersed himself in clothing design and production with no prior knowledge—and looked to experts in finance and business processes for the expertise he needed. Trisha Rae, who started the Christmas is for Children non-profit over 20 years ago, decided she needed to do more to help children and their parents have a special Christmas, but had no idea how to keep it going at first.

I've had many times in my life when I had no clue what I was doing and decided I'd have to figure it out. I progressed pretty quickly in my career so I had many times when I felt I was "in over my head." I started a consulting business when I had no prior exposure to running a business, much less when sales directly determined my income. I wanted to write a book and had no clue how to do it or how to get an agent, and I discovered becoming an author was completely different from anything I had done before. When we concluded that the best path to ensure PeopleResults was sustainable and continued to grow—I knew nothing about exploring acquisitions or finding investors. In these situations, listening and learning from others helped me keep going.

Gretchen Seay, Co-Founder and Managing Director of Clearsight Advisors started this investment banking firm in the middle of the 2011 financial crisis—not the best time to start a new venture. She and her other two co-founders had been exploring starting this firm for about three years. They used that time to educate themselves and build their capability so they'd be ready when the time was right. In those three years of learning, they not only got smarter and grew their capabilities, but they even redefined the planned services and offerings. This prep time helped but didn't stop them from reaching their goal, even when starting the business, especially in that market, was full of risks.

Gretchen explained, "It was still a big leap for me to start this business even with co-founders. At the time, I was a single parent with young children. I wanted to make the right decision. I was trying to decide what to do, so I called my Mom for advice. She said, 'In life, you usually don't regret what you did as much as what you *didn't* do.' Her words gave me so much clarity. I knew if it didn't work, I could go back to PWC. This decision could be reversed if I ever wanted to. I knew I had to take the risk."

Before we started the business, we made sure we knew what we wanted—and also what we didn't.

—Gretchen Seay

SIZE UP THE CHANGE

Not every change is the same. What you need to learn or know for an organization-wide transformation is wildly different than changing how your small team communicates with each other. Situational awareness is essential when you set your learning goals. You can get to what is required of you—but first, start by assessing "what does this specific change need?"

In simple terms, change shows up in three different general categories:

- *Cultural*: if your change impacts the culture, you will have more significant headwinds if it collides with "how we've always done it"
- *Situational*: if your change is situational, it is tied to one specific circumstance and is more isolated or targeted and may be easier to contain or manage
- *Individual*: if an individual has an impact on your change, consider how to address their impact upfront

Let's explore each.

A *cultural change* is the hardest because it takes more time, requires more commitment and sponsorship, and there's more to learn if you are the change champion. The example of data analytics in baseball and Billy Beane is a full-blown cultural change still discussed in sports today. At the time, the Oakland A's had scouts who watched with their eyes and drew conclusions. The data revolution meant that analytics and information led you to answers, minimizing or at least reshaping an entire Major League Baseball function. It was a very belated culture change for Augusta National, home of the Masters Golf Tournament, to finally allow women members—but not until 2012. Or, Fiona Grant who championed partner benefits at Accenture when very few Fortune 500 organizations even considered it. Cultural changes take a coalition to create movement.

Situational means the change is more specific. Examples might be combining two groups into one, expanding the services of your non-profit, or creating a women's mentoring group. Because it's more targeted, your learning areas may be easier to get your arms around.

Individual means you have one person to consider who is critical to making the change happen. If this person is a full-time critic, you'll have to learn to manage around or through them. Identify these critics proactively upfront and get their input early and often so they can't wait until the end to voice their concerns. Understand and consider their style and expectations early. I once worked for a leader who just wanted the headlines and summary; however, he also wanted to see if you knew the details. So, I learned to share the detailed analysis in advance that I know he never actually read and be prepared for a few in-depth questions. Once he was confident we had done our homework and a thorough assessment—he was on board with just the headlines. But he wanted to see we weren't skimming the surface. So, I always considered his style for any recommended change.

If you know who these individuals are, you can learn how to adapt to their style, listen, and determine if they have concerns about the change— or just always have concerns.

CULTURAL TRENDS AND UNDERCURRENTS

As you focus on what you need to know, look around you at the culture and expectations that will affect you. These are common undercurrents and trends to consider upfront and incorporate into your learning plan.

Meaningful Work

Your change will have wings if it matters to you and helps others find meaning in their work. In my research, I discovered that Wave Makers are motivated to achieve goals beyond their own personal success. They knew their "why," which kept them going, and kept others committed too. They have a passion for their change.

Guwan Jones, the former head of Diversity and Inclusion at Baylor, Scott & White, connected diversity to patient care and she shared how she developed a passion for her work and cause. Guwan said, "While I was in school working on my bachelor's, the world was facing HIV and AIDS. And I wanted to take care of those folks. At first, I went to school to become a physician. I worked in a clinic and found out that I really want to help people, but I also want to have kids and more control of my life. I didn't want to live off of a pager. I learned that there are a lot of different ways that you can take care of people. So, seeing people diagnosed with HIV or AIDS and having a really hard time made me see the broader community out there. It's also part of the community I live in. I'm African American; I've seen my family and friends really suffer from diseases that we could probably do a better job of taking care of. And so, a lot of what I do, I think, is selfish. It is fulfilling something that deep down I need to fulfill."

Guwan fulfilled this purpose through her commitment to translating diversity and workforce analytics so that patients ultimately connect with caregivers like them. She kept her passion for quality patient care and made it a core part of her work, regardless of her position.

In his search for meaning, Rich Sheridan, changed the course of his career and his life when he founded Menlo Innovations and a very different way of creating software. Rich said, "We all seek purpose. I think we are, by and large, wired as individuals and as communities to leave the world a better place than we found it. I know it's hard, and the world is conspiring against me, but that's my intent. These days, particularly since the world is so complex, we have to do it in concert with others. There are very few individual heroes anymore."

After much learning and searching, Rich had ideas for a significant change at the software company where he worked. He began asking the developers on the team he led to work in pairs, partner with sponsors, and rapidly deliver working software at least every two weeks. His team was initially skeptical but believed in the change after they experienced the difference firsthand. The results surpassed Rich's expectations, and he took what he learned as a VP of R&D and cofounded Menlo Innovations with one focused purpose: *Ending human suffering in the world as it relates to technology.*™ That's another way of saying that technology should be simple, responsive, and easy to use rather than a painful obstacle.

Human beings are wired to work on something bigger than themselves.

—Rich Sheridan

Wave Makers fulfill their potential by adding meaning to their work and lives. Bruce Ballengee, founder and former CEO of Pariveda Solutions, touched on this point: "What does it take for a person to completely fulfill their potential? It means that at some point in their life, they're going to have to be about helping other people. Because that is what brings fulfillment. You can't help yourself without helping other people. It's becoming a trusted advisor, having a network of people who trust you, and being engaged in serving your community. All of these come together in a servant leader."

Bite-Sized Communication

We expect information to be short and concise in our fast-paced, impatient world. There is growing evidence that social media and changing technology are rewiring our brains so that we have shorter attention spans than ever before.

Dr. Gloria Mark, a professor of informatics at the University of California, Irvine, studies how digital media affects our lives. In her book *Attention Span: A Groundbreaking Way to Restore Balance, Happiness and Productivity*, Mark explains how decades of research have tracked the decline of the ability to focus.

Dr. Mark shared, "In 2004, we measured the average attention on a screen to be 2½ minutes. Some years later, we found attention spans to be about 75 seconds. Now we find people can only pay attention to one screen for an average of 47 seconds."[5]

> Don't put all the dessert on the table at once. Bring a few things out at a time. Then, test it and make sure it works. As your changes have uptake, then introduce something else new. Pace yourself.
>
> —Mark Benton

Hyperconnected individuals are increasing the trend for short and fast. They are almost always connected by mobile technology and use multiple sources simultaneously. This continuous loop of working and engagement is assumed.

Social media is based on snackable or bite-sized information, and our increased multitasking drives the need for just the headlines. This short and quick, sample mentality is a trend in nearly every facet of modern life.

Bite-size content doesn't replace our need for depth, however. We just want to dive deeper only when we choose. Otherwise, the headlines will do.

Wave Maker Joe Nussbaum started The Big Event, a student-run service project, at Texas A&M. In the first year, Nussbaum and his team spoke with hundreds of student leaders and committees and gained their commitment to both participating and encouraging others. He got the initial commitment by sharing snackable content—just enough to get them interested and involved.

Joe said, "When you start a change, present it in a way that is very simple and easy to understand. You don't have much time to get their attention. Make it a simple thing to agree to." At this early point, you are requesting involvement—ongoing commitment will come in time.

But don't let the shorter attention spans and need for speed affect your expectations for results. Change takes time. Be patient and persistent while understanding that you have a very distracted and busy audience on your hands.

What does this trend toward brief content mean for you and your change? Here are some suggestions:

- Get attention for your change early.
- Share your story in bite-sized pieces. Dribble out information that builds interest and commitment over time rather than too much in one sitting. You can go into more detail later, but start with the headlines and purpose to build interest and then phase in more detail.
- Know how your audience prefers to consume information and collaborate. Assume that the majority will appreciate short and sweet in this busy, distracted world.
- Yet, take the time you need to tell your story. Balance short & sweet with meaning. Ensure the "why" and the impact on the individual are clear.

Personal Endorsements

Research tells us that we most value the recommendations of those we know much more than campaigns or packaged communications. As a result, companies hope that a friend or influencer's recommendations shared on social media will encourage you to check them out. Influencer marketing is growing over three times faster than normal ad spending because we view these recommendations more like personal endorsements. Not quite like a good friend, but someone we follow and find interesting.

Personal requests and appeals can change behavior. A few years ago, my friend Laurie Axford asked me why I wasn't part of a local women's community service group. I had often considered it, but there was no impetus to get involved. I was already very busy and not looking for new commitments to add to my schedule. But Laurie called and encouraged me to get involved. She said she thought I could make a real contribution and emphasized the group's impact on the community. Then, she said, "Would you like to come with me to a meeting next week and see what you think?" She came and picked me up. Guess what? Between her appeal and her making it so easy to go—no big commitment—I joined. However, I would never have gone without her personal invitation.

Following are some steps that will help you capitalize, in your wave, on the trend toward personal recommendations:

- Identify the key influencers and involve them early. Their agreement and interest will affect others.
- Identify a plan for positive word of mouth and recommendations, such as a change network or advocates.
- Don't overly rely on formal communications, such as presentations, speeches, and one-way communication.
- Remember, when you consider momentum builders for your change, one of them could be the involvement and engagement of the right people.
- Make it easy to act on a personal recommendation.

Human Connection

The more time we spend on our phones and in front of our screens, the more notable and unique our personal and human interactions become. And teams are more virtual than ever, relying more on technology to connect us. These changes in technology and ways of working have lowered the number of in-person connections we have. And, even when we are together in person, technology has our attention. The family out for dinner and the kids on their phones and iPads is the norm today.

Texts or emails are more standard than a call or in-person conversation. Handwritten notes are a lost art. At a recent client workshop, we all shared our most memorable celebrations of success. No one mentioned the salary increase or the company announcement. We all told stories of the personal notes or calls from people we respected or the special acknowledgment at a team gathering. It reminded me that these simple human connections must be valued and remembered in any change.

I am emphasizing the human connection not because of nostalgia but as a reminder that it may be necessary if you need memorable or high impact. Like you, I value efficiency and typically prefer a text or quick email; however, if you want others to engage and feel part of a change—the fastest may not be best.

Mark Benton, currently a VP in HR at McKesson and who previously redefined careers in R&D at PepsiCo, shared the importance of human connection in his wave. Mark said, "I think one of our biggest factors in building momentum was being close to those most impacted by the change. And that meant I had to physically get out of my office—get on an airplane, get in a car, and find time to meet in person." Mark added, "We're in such a fast-paced world, and there is a tendency to communicate through a device. You can't underestimate the power of being there in person."

I also have also learned the value of learning via dialogue and interaction. When I started my business, and we continued to grow, I learned a lot from research, YouTube, and reading. But, when I think of the information that most affected my decisions, it was conversations with wise experts who could bring what they knew and apply it to my specific situation. This interactive exchange had the most impact on me and my success.

For example, when I started PeopleResults, I was concerned because I was a novice at sales or business development and felt it didn't fit who I was. At Accenture, I had been part of big teams working on new client opportunities, but this was a much smaller scale and felt completely different. I was anxious about this new responsibility as I knew when you start a business, you have to be out in the market and generate revenue. I had a long lunch with a mentor and shared my lack of confidence. I have returned to her wise words many times since. She said, "It's pretty simple. People buy from people they like and they trust. Trust means you know what you are doing and want to help them." This made everything clearer. I could do both! I did want to help my clients, be part of getting them recognized for great work, and tackle big problems. I didn't need to become someone I wasn't. It was this in-person conversation and human connection that reshaped my thinking and moved me forward.

As in-person conversations have become the exception rather than the rule, these traditional methods of communication are more unique and memorable in any change. Here are some options for incorporating the human connection into your change:

- Know when an in-person connection rather than a virtual one is essential. Key sponsors and those not on board may need personal attention.
- Remember the personal appeal to get involved, as it will have more impact than a group email or post.
- Consider using techniques counter to trends that will be noticed. Examples may include a personal note or a phone call to check in or say thank you.
- Look for other unique ideas that will engage and involve others that aren't typical in your ongoing workday.

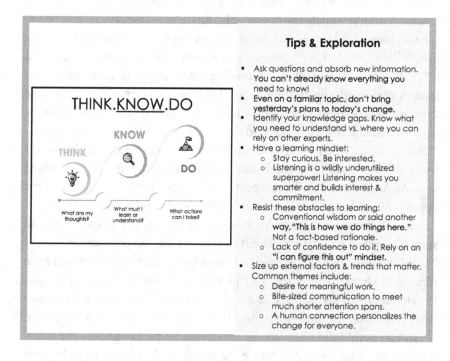

Tips & Exploration

- Ask questions and absorb new information. You can't already know everything you need to know!
- Even on a familiar topic, don't bring yesterday's plans to today's change.
- Identify your knowledge gaps. Know what you need to understand vs. where you can rely on other experts.
- Have a learning mindset:
  - Stay curious. Be interested.
  - Listening is a wildly underutilized superpower! Listening makes you smarter and builds interest & commitment.
- Resist these obstacles to learning:
  - Conventional wisdom or said another way, "This is how we do things here." Not a fact-based rationale.
  - Lack of confidence to do it. Rely on an "I can figure this out" mindset.
- Size up external factors & trends that matter. Common themes include:
  - Desire for meaningful work.
  - Bite-sized communication to meet much shorter attention spans.
  - A human connection personalizes the change for everyone.

THINK TIME

1. What do you need to learn that you don't understand today?
2. What is your strategy for getting smarter on this topic?
3. What expertise do you need that will require relying on others (the topic is too complex or requires more knowledge than you can obtain)?
4. How will you get this needed expertise? Who can you involve to fill this gap?
5. What external trends will likely affect your change besides those mentioned in this chapter?
6. What trends do you need to better understand? How can you gain that knowledge?
7. What is your learning plan for starting or leading this change?

NOTES

1 Leon Seltzer, *Psychology Today*, July 2023: "Curiosity Is Invaluable: Can We Lose It as We Age?"
2 Stephen R. Covey, *Seven Habits of Highly Successful People* (New York: Free Press, 1989).
3 John Kenneth Galbraith, *The Affluent Society* (Boston, MS Houghton Mifflin, 1958).
4 Michael Lewis, *Moneyball* (W.W. Norton & Company, 2004).
5 Dr. Gloria Mark, *Attention Span: A Groundbreaking Way to Restore Balance, Happiness & Productivity* (Hanover Press, 2023); CNN article by Sandee LaMotte, May 30, 2023, "Your Attention Span Is Shrinking, Studies Say. Here's How to Stay Focused."

Part 3

What You Do

4

Starting Your Wave

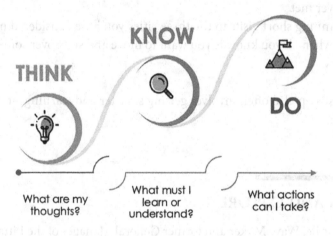

In Chapter 2, we examined the ultimate driver in deciding to start a wave. You've now identified the internal thoughts and habits most likely to get in your way and learned new ways to manage them. We also discussed identifying what you need to learn. Now that you are ready to act, let's look at how to start.

I've avoided using the word "steps" because it implies that change is orderly and sequential—or there is a formula. There isn't. Instead, a wave has a natural flow, with dependencies that overlap and happen concurrently. Think of starting any change like dance steps, where you improvise rather than marching through a predictable process.

DOI: 10.4324/9781032715339-7

We know the most challenging part of anything big or important is the very first step. We talk repeatedly about the mindset of beginning. Focus on "What can I do right now?" The first step may be very small, but it will start the dominoes that lead to progress. Here are examples of deciding to start that can make a big difference over time:

- Going for a 15-minute walk because it was doable and on your path to a healthier lifestyle
- Scheduling a meeting with a successful entrepreneur when you want to start a business but have no clue where to begin
- Blocking time on your calendar to start working on the strategic project you've been given and keep putting off
- Coming up with a plan for the first day with your new team you've never met
- Planning short visits to the three cities you have considered moving to when all you know is you want to move and start over somewhere new

Your first step also often involves getting smarter and learning—but with a deadline.

LISTEN AND EXPLORE

Clint Hurdle, Wave Maker and former General Manager of the Pittsburgh Pirates, said each clubhouse and team is a little different. He described his first step starting as a new manager: "You ask a lot of questions, and then you really listen. It's a new environment with new players, why wouldn't you listen? Do you have all of the answers? Is there nothing left to know? Listening is gathering real information before deciding what to do."

Understand the situation from more than your perspective. Listen for what is most important, matters most, is working today and what isn't. Understand the unseen opportunity before you start the change.

Before you create ideas, comprehend the world around you:

- Trends and changes that will affect the future
- Unmet or unspoken needs

- Your goals for the future
- Paths to progress and movement forward—even if small at first

Cynthia Young, a Wave Maker who changed her organization's culture through a passion for servant leadership, said, "I accepted the fact that I could be wrong and just listened. This is how I really understood the people and the issues." This point is important because you need to have a full understanding that your wave is needed, important, meaningful, or provides an opportunity.

> **I had no fear of asking questions. Because I knew I didn't have all the answers.**
>
> **—Guwan Jones**

Wave Maker Brett Hurt, the cofounder of Bazaarvoice, explained that he had to thank Neal Kocurek, an Austin community leader and president and CEO of St. David's Healthcare System, whom he sought out for advice a few months before Kocurek passed away. Brett listened for wisdom and insights on two business options he was considering. Brett said: "Over lunch, I told Neal about both of my ideas for my next business. He said, 'I don't know anything about either one of the industries. But I can tell you're more passionate about the open community idea [Bazaarvoice], and you have many relationships in that industry. You are probably underestimating how valuable all of that knowledge is. You'll soon realize how important all of those connections are to you.'"

Brett said that his answer became crystal clear after that lunch with a person he respected but didn't know well. The insights he gained were not based on market needs but on how he personally could be most successful in filling it. His first step became clearer.

Listening won't always give you all the answers, especially if your idea is new. Steve Jobs, the premier innovator, once said, "It's really hard to design products by focus groups. Often, people don't know what they want until you show it to them."

Like Brett, listen for information and meaning that you can translate for your wave rather than looking for precise answers. Your idea may evolve and become different than what you first imagined.

KNOW YOUR WHY

Your wave needs a bigger purpose and meaning so you stay motivated, build interest, and, most importantly, do something that matters. Consider the difference between the entrepreneur who starts his business solely because he sees a gap in the market and the one who sees the gap but is driven by a desire to help customers be healthier and live longer. Of course, market needs and financial opportunities are essential for the viability of any business. Still, purpose will make your wave sustainable for your customers and you.

Wave Maker Bob Wright's creation of the bigBANG! community event in Dallas caught on not because it was a great event—though it was—but because it was built upon connecting a new generation of leaders to needs in the Dallas community. The Eli Group's Leadership Lab for executive women has been successful for over a decade because it creates a safe forum for women leaders to learn and help each other find their version of success.

Many business leaders today depend on financial outcomes as the rallying cry they share with others. Of course, financials are at the core of how you run a business and evaluate success. But you must define the meaning and purpose behind the numbers before others will commit and know how they can contribute.

When I told Tory Johnson, a successful entrepreneur and regular contributor on Good Morning America, I wanted to write a book about starting and leading change. Her questions pushed my thinking. She asked me, "Why do you want to write a book—what do you hope to achieve?" I answered that it was on my bucket list and something I had always wanted to do. She asked again, "But why is it on your bucket list?" She pressed further, "What do you hope the book will do for you or your business?' 'What impact do you want it to have on your life and work?" She explained it would take a lot of work when I already had a demanding schedule. Tory explained that some write a book to engage new clients and grow their business, to be a requested speaker, or to be a known expert. What was my purpose? I found myself mumbling answers at first. But I left with my homework. I needed more clarity on my purpose—what mattered to me and what didn't. I realized that I'd learned a lot in my work and wanted to share it to help others, including my clients. Yes, I wanted to be seen as an expert, but I wanted to share my experiences and examples to give others ideas on how to start their change. This answer would be my guide and purpose to keep going—when I knew it wouldn't be easy.

> **You have to be really clear about what you want to do and why. You have to know your 'why.'**
>
> —Tory Johnson

At work, finding meaning can show up in different ways. For example, I led a healthcare leadership workshop, and participants shared a great example of how meaning fueled their work and willingness to change. The company needed to attract more quality nurses in a very competitive market. In examining their "why," they realized they were using their internal job descriptions, built for job leveling and pay, to explain the role to external candidates. They decided to return to the core reason nurses are nurses—they want to save lives and improve the health of others. This realization set in motion a series of changes in how they described and marketed their opportunities for nurses. This return to what nurses valued led this talent acquisition team to a new way of connecting and it significantly improved their results.

A change with meaning is sustainable—values that won't be out of vogue next year. For example, a financial analyst's purpose may be to help her clients become financially secure so they can live their dream, a nonprofit leader may want to improve literacy in his city, and a business analyst's purpose may be to simplify complex business decisions. Think about your change and your purpose together because your purpose may lead you to your wave.

Wave Maker Lindsay Pender, a nurse, improved infant care in the neonatal ICU by importing ideas from her previous employer, a large metropolitan hospital, to her new smaller hospital. Lindsay's simple purpose was to help the babies: "I knew that not everyone would agree with my ideas or want to change, but that if I—and we—kept our attention on the babies, we could find a way to make progress."

The "why" is essential to starting your wave. Integrated it into everything you say and do so that others remember it—and so you do too.

TAKE YOUR FIRST STEP

The challenge is knowing your "why"—your aspiration before you start. The translation from goal to action is the superpower of any Wave Maker.

As BJ Fogg, PhD, shares in Tiny Habits, "Humans are dreamers by nature, so we've all got a few moon shots tucked in our back pocket at all times. But that's often where they stay—in part because we are tripped up by fickle motivation. So how do we pull aspirations out of our pockets and start making them happen without relying on motivation?"

Motivation comes and goes. You are excited about the new idea, but after a few weeks, your enthusiasm fades. The new plan for eating healthy foods or weekly check-ins with your team will run out of steam if you rely solely on motivation. Instead, focus on changing your behavior and small actions to build momentum.

Wave Makers are predisposed to action, even when they don't have all the answers. Beginning before you know every step is hard for those of us who want to know, be right, and have all the answers. And these small steps aren't dependent upon motivation.

Mark Benton, a VP of HR at McKesson shared his view on getting started, "Starting or leading a change can be learned, but it's not an easy skill to be taught. You can provide the right tools and training, but it still comes down to a person deciding to take action at that moment."

Many of us earned our reputations and progressed in business because we are problem solvers and fixers. And, if you have perfectionist tendencies, it's time to put them in the drawer. Remember that starting a wave isn't the same as earning an A+ or clearing your to-do list. It's creating momentum toward your goal and engaging others to be part of it. It's not a command-and-control effort. As a result, information gathering early is essential—even before you have all the answers.

Lois Melbourne, Wave Maker, co-creator, and former CEO of Aquire, shared the tension between gathering the facts and taking action. Lois said,

> I want to learn and feel like I can make a very educated decision. I read everything. Ask tons of questions. Do the research. Don't wait for perfect data—or even all of the data. When people think, "I just need a little more information," that drives me up the wall. But at the same time, I don't make uneducated decisions. I feel like gut instincts come from assimilating a lot

of information and then making the decision that you need to—even if, at that specific moment, you don't have all of the data. You know enough about the environment to be able to make an educated guess. That is enough.

In *Tiny Habits*, Hogg explains the difference between aspirations and new behavior that moves you forward, "A behavior is something you can do right now or at another specific point in time. You can turn off your phone. You can eat a carrot. You can open a textbook and read five pages. These are actions that you can do at any given moment. You cannot suddenly get better sleep. You cannot lose 12 pounds at dinner tonight. You can only achieve aspirations and outcomes over time if you execute the right specific behaviors. I've found that people don't naturally think in terms of specific behaviors and this tendency trips up almost everyone."[1]

Two essential reasons why changing your behavior and specific short-term actions will help you begin before you have everything planned:

1. Months three and four of your plan will change by the time you get there anyway. You'll be a lot smarter by then. Plus, others will bring new ideas that make your plan better.
2. Your change will never happen if it is just an aspiration or idea without changing daily behavior and action.

Wave Maker Brett Hurt, an entrepreneur and co-creator of Bazaarvoice, shared the importance of movement. He said, "You've got to get going. Surround yourself with other people who are incredibly passionate about your cause and move. If you have a dream, you have to get moving, or it's never going to happen. Now, if I'm looking to invest in an entrepreneur, for example, I'm looking for motion—someone who is really going after their dream and is passionate about it. They can approach it differently than me or have a different personality than me, but they have to be going after it. Let's get going. If you really believe in it, why not? Why aren't you moving?"

Motion creates motion. Momentum creates momentum.

—Brett Hurt

Also, you can't realize most changes alone unless you are the only one who needs to change! Change isn't a solo sport. Inviting others to be part of your wave—especially at the beginning—is essential. They'll make you smarter, and this is how the wave becomes "our" wave, not just "your" wave.

Almost all the Wave Makers began sharing their ideas before they had all the answers. It was how they got smarter, built momentum, and eventually a community that cared.

Wave Maker Bob Wright, a leader of the Dallas Social Venture Partners (DSVP) and creator of The bigBANG!, started the idea but quickly let others be part of developing it. Bob and a few partners wanted the event to be like no other—no conference with a static agenda, no talking heads, and no formal event. It had to be something that new generations in the community wanted to be part of, with the hope of their continued commitment.

Bob described how they started: "We lived by the belief that we can't own and control this. We have to turn loose of the steering wheel and let others be part of shaping it. We crowdsourced the creation of this experience because we wanted a broader circle to feel responsibility for it."

Bob created a few informal events to start the discussion. He and his partners invited about 25 select social innovators to a discussion and asked for their participation. The invitation told them to invite anyone they felt should be included. Seventy-five people showed up for their first get-together. That meeting resulted in four Spark Clubs, idea-generating groups, which all contributed and helped develop the bigBANG!, shaping how it would work and its goal for community impact.

Bob and his partners at DSVP created a wave that people wanted to be part of and were involved in creating. They defined the intent upfront and knew their goals, but they let others create the how and the what. This example is illuminating because they realized it wasn't just about the event but about building a longer-term commitment to the cause. They let others help create and run it and achieved more than they had imagined.

Brooke Averick, a well-known social media podcast host, Tik Toker, and comedy creator, said her unhappiness caused her to start her change. She was a preschool teacher in Pennsylvania who became a teacher because it was the obvious next step for her—not because it was what she really wanted to do. She had always been interested in media and comedy. It all came together with the small decision to start reading from her old diaries on TikTok during the pandemic at the urging of her sister. She quickly had some videos go viral, and while she didn't have many followers at first, her initial success was her signal to try something new that fit her goals.

In our social world, Brooke found the motivation to start from dissatisfaction with her current life, and the change began with a small experiment—not a big life plan. Then, the path slowly started to appear in front of her. Brooke said, "We can often rely too much on 'What will others like? What will they approve of?' in any job—but especially when you provide content out into the world. Brooke said she has learned to always go to the important question of, 'What do I like?' and 'What is interesting to *me*?' rather than constantly guessing what others will like." This belief in herself has helped her know the right next step.

Brooke also explained that she is now comfortable living and learning from each day and is willing to let an idea or goal evolve. She added, "So many times, we are constantly asking each other and ourselves, 'What do you want to do next?' Instead, I'm thinking about 'now'. I'm doing this well 'right now'—not 'what am I going to do next?'"

> **When you are so focused on the next thing, you miss other important things right in front of you.**
>
> —Brooke Averick

FIND YOUR IDEA CIRCLE

Finding your Idea Circle doesn't mean finding others who are just like you, think like you, or know what you know. Connect with others who *want what you want*—that is enough for now. Find people who, like you, want to create the best learning environment for disadvantaged children, customers to be integrally involved in product creation, or are committed to the advancement of women. Start developing a connection with those who share your passion and purpose because those people have a built-in interest in your change.

In Brooke's case, as she shifted from preschool teacher to a social content creator, she realized she wanted to be around others who understood her work and world. She knew she wouldn't get this back in Philadelphia. So, she decided to move to LA, but with an experimental, "Let's see how it goes" mindset.

Brooke shared, "Why not go? If I go out there and I hate it, I don't have to stay. So, I got an Airbnb, and I was like, let's see how it goes for two months. If it's good, it's good. If it's not, you can always leave. But it ended up working. Once I was in LA, it felt good right away because even the people around me who were just friends and not in the industry had a level of understanding about what I did that people in Philadelphia or somewhere else didn't have. And there are more people in the industry here who you get to meet and connect with, and ultimately, that's what led to a podcast I do now. It was a great decision that, at first, looked like a snap decision. But it wasn't like that."

In Brooke's case, she knew what she wanted, but having the right circle around her helped her expand her dream.

You are looking for a few people for your Idea Circle to:

- Help you determine how to solve the problem or seize the opportunity
- Share ideas
- Be engaged from the start
- Be there for you to provide support, partnership, and collaboration
- Help you spread the word and build an engaged community around your idea and work

When you identify your Idea Circle, include those who know what you don't know. Talk with people who look at the world differently than you to learn and test your assumptions.

If your wave depends upon new technology, you'll probably need someone with technology knowledge and expertise in your Idea Circle. Early on, you'll know your expertise gaps which we discussed in Chapter 3. You don't need a detailed solution yet, but you'll need contributions from someone who understands the possibilities and gives ideas that will eventually work.

You must trust those in your informal Idea Circle, though they don't need to be your best friends. You want the right mix of needed knowledge and passion for the issues you care about most. One of the best leadership teams I was part of had diverse personalities and styles. We trusted one another but didn't go to lunch together, and we weren't best friends. We did respect one another, and I knew we had the smarts and the commitment to take on the big challenges in front of us. That was enough.

Bob Wright, a Wave Maker who started the bigBANG! to connect a new generation of leaders to the Dallas community, said, "People asked what to expect when they came to the bigBANG! We said that you should expect that this will be the one place where you will see the suits talking to the creatives and people standing around in jeans and bow ties. It was going to be an eclectic mix of people. We had no idea how it would play, but people (for reasons I still don't understand) just trusted us."

> **I don't think we knew exactly what we wanted at first, but we knew we wanted to do something significant.**
>
> **—Bob Wright**

A few years ago, domestic partner benefits were the exception to most corporate benefit plans. Fiona Grant, who started a wave that led to Accenture offering domestic partner benefits, shared how they got started. She said the energy behind their recommendations began after IBM came out with domestic partner benefits. Coincidentally, a few weeks later, the new Accenture CEO said he was behind bold change for the organization. Fiona heard that "bold change" message and felt the time was right to act!

Fiona said, "I went to a senior leader at Accenture and said I really want to make a go at domestic partner benefits. Can we retry? Because it had been tried in the past, but unsuccessfully. We got a core team of people and started meeting regularly to put together our business case. Richard (a senior financial leader) is a very strategic thinker. He advised us on how to create the right business case and get the facts we'd need. You have to have a little core group. If you were by yourself, it would be spectacularly hard."

> **Find a partner or two to do this with. Starting a change can be very lonely.**
>
> **—Bob Wright**

PEOPLE SUPPORT WHAT THEY HELP CREATE

You may have used the expression "on the back of a napkin" to refer to ideas drafted informally. I found this casual dialogue essential for building ideas for change. Informal give-and-take allows others to be part of creating the concept, which is very different from shopping your idea to others. In my interviews with Wave Makers, I heard over and over that their idea first started over a glass of wine, on a long flight home, or in an informal conversation.

Surprisingly, literally, no one I interviewed said their change began in a formal brainstorming meeting, at a leadership summit, or even during a team meeting. Yet, in business, we rely heavily on these more formal structured forums to set strategy and make decisions.

This back-of-the-napkin mentality works because it's an informal discussion with just two or three interested people, with no predetermined outcome. You are creating something new with others rather than trying to convince someone your idea is right. And these discussions offer a safe place to share unfiltered and untested ideas. The Wave Makers I spoke with often used language like, "I have an idea I'd like to share to see what you think about it."

As Guwan Jones said when she was talking about her new ideas on diversity at Baylor, Scott & White, "I always approached my discussions with 'Here's what I'm thinking.'" This approach was her way of letting others know she wanted to explore the topic and was open to other ideas. It's much easier to test and create your change when you aren't recommending yet—you are noodling and letting others be part of shaping your idea.

> You're in trouble when it starts to be all about your idea.
>
> —Bob Wright

Dan Roam, author of *The Back of the Napkin: Solving Problems and Selling Ideas with Pictures,* describes the experience of informal creation like this: "The reaction that you get from an audience is like magic, because they are with you, seeing the idea being built as opposed to coming in with a set of charts already prepared."[2] Think how different it is when someone says, "Let me show you the answer," versus telling you, "I have some ideas and would love to hear what you think," then invites you to shape the ideas together.[3]

Going into a discussion with no previously defined answer lets two or three people build on one another's thoughts instead of working toward an answer already in mind. While writing this book, I have had countless back-of-the-napkin conversations; each gave me a fresh idea or new way to think.

Exchange ideas with those with valuable perspectives—especially if those perspectives differ from yours. This kind of sharing can have an amazing effect on your change, activating and engaging first believers because they helped create the idea.

KEEP IT SIMPLE

Simple, clear goals will help you keep your focus and make it much easier to involve others. Simplicity is essential in this world of short attention spans and volumes of information. However, creating clarity is more challenging than including everything but the kitchen sink. Fight the urge to favor complexity over simplicity, even though complicated plans can make us feel like the expert and reinforce our importance.

Thomas McQueen leads a very successful legal firm in Austin specializing in mergers and acquisitions. Thomas and his colleagues are experts on very detailed legal matters, yet his clients must understand the transaction. As a client of Thomas and his team at QS&S Legal, I witnessed firsthand their ability to translate and simply communicate with me what mattered.

Thomas shared that it's more than just style; you must fully understand the content and prepare to simplify it for others. He said, "When translating complex to simple, I think preparation is critical. I don't believe you can fake it till you make it. You've got to know the details and be fully prepared. For me, that knowledge is what gives me confidence that I can simplify it for others. I've got to know all the documents better than the other side. Even if they're the other side's documents, I've got to know them backward and forward. Being fully prepared gives me the quiet comfort and confidence that I know what I can tease out. What's really important here? We've looked around the corner as best as we can and can simplify it."

A simple goal can make decisions easier, make planning more straightforward, and help leave behind unnecessary extras.

I like Alan Siegel and Irene Etzkorn's framework in their book *Simple: Conquering the Crisis of Complexity*. The authors believe that there are three elements of simplicity:

- "*Empathize*: understand others' needs and expectations
- *Distill*: boil down and customize what's being offered to meet needs
- *Clarify*: make the offering easier to understand, use, and provide a benefit

Empathizing and listening are essential for achieving simplicity and connecting. Distilling and clarifying seem more intuitive, but empathizing connects simplicity to the real meaning. You can't realize simplicity if you don't empathize with your audience. The best task force survey or detailed process analysis isn't enough."[4]

Thomas Queen explained the importance of listening to simplify communications. He said, "I think you listen and do an inventory of the client's objectives, their knowledge base, and risk profile. Understand what this person cares about, how they prefer to communicate, and their communication style. Some people are verbal, and some people prefer written communication. Some people need to hear it three times. You really are trying to understand. And so I think we probably tailor our communications and counsel per the client."

> This qualitative understanding comes from asking questions, being observant, and also knowing what a client isn't telling you.
>
> —Thomas Queen

Emma Scheffler, who started Insulin Angels while a high school sophomore, knew the fear that children and parents feel when they are diagnosed with diabetes because she had been there. Parents have fears and questions like, "Will my child be able to be active, play sports, and just be like the other kids?" Insulin Angels paired high school students with kids just diagnosed with diabetes to show them it's possible to carry on with active, healthy lives. Emma's empathetic response was to use the fears she and her family experienced to create a charity that addressed other families' deepest needs. Emma's change led with empathy.

Empathy takes imagination, sensitivity, and a willingness to look under the surface. In business, these can unfortunately be grouped with the "soft stuff" and slip down your priority list. Yet empathy is essential for finding your simple message and creating your desired impact.

Wave Maker Trisha Rae, who started Christmas is for Children, explained a fundamental principle when asking volunteers to help. She said, "You have to honor and respect others' time. Keep your requests simple and specific. Make it easy for people to contribute. If you keep it simple, it's much easier for people to decide to get involved."

Keep that underlying need of your audience in mind, and use empathy to ensure you have a simple, clear, and compelling goal that fits your audience.

> **A person who leads a change has to have empathy for who they're impacting.**
>
> **—Mark Benton**

Thomas Queen shared a great analogy on making it simple, "I think a lot of what we do as M&A experts is more like the surgeon. I may only have five minutes with you by your bed, but I've got to be able to communicate to you and your loved ones exactly in plain English what's going on. It's super complex, and it's our job to simplify it into what matters to you. That's how I've always thought about what we do."

Share with Everyone

Many Wave Makers described talking with "hundreds of people" about their ideas. They viewed themselves as the personal advocate and interest builder for the project. No one mentioned the fantastic campaign or the jaw-dropping presentation; it all came back to personal conversations and recommendations from people they trusted.

Share your ideas. Ask for other people's thoughts. Share with everyone what you are up to. For example, if you are changing the hiring process at your company, start early by telling everyone the benefit of a transformed recruiting experience that creates future customers rather than just pre-screening out candidates. Decide who can react to your ideas and help you learn more.

Allen Stephenson, a Wave Maker who founded Southern Tide while a college student, shared his first actions and where he chose to spend his energies: "I stopped my social life, but I kept using my same social skills. I just started using them in a different way. I met anyone I could who might know someone or wanted to help in any way. I'd ask them for advice or ideas, and I helped them any way I could too. It was very difficult for me to process it all because I had to meet so many people."

Allen continued, "I talked to people who used to own apparel manufacturing companies, financial people, and so many others. I was taking people out to lunch like crazy—every day, like three, four, or five people. And some of them are still involved today. Obviously, I didn't find all of them myself, but that's how I did it. I didn't and don't know how to do all this stuff, but I did know how to say, 'This is the vision, the dream. We're going to do this and have clothes in the way that I'm describing, and we can do this together.'"

I had a similar mindset when I started my business because I had so much to learn. I met with dozens of people individually and told them my plans. I asked for their advice and words of wisdom about how to get my business off the ground. Gibbs Mood, a successful business leader and a mentor at Accenture, told me, "Don't get too clever and overthink it. Just tell everyone you meet what you are doing and your goals for your business. You never know what ideas you'll hear or where those conversations will lead. It's hands-down the best way to get others interested in your plans."

He was right, though his advice was counter to much of the conventional marketing wisdom I heard at the time.

> **Never assume that once is enough. Repeat it over and over again until you think you have said it to everyone a million times.**
>
> —Joe Nussbaum

Lois Melbourne, co-creator and former CEO of Aquire, accelerated her company's growth by engaging in social media to build relationships and a community within the software industry. She joined discussion groups, contributed to countless blogs, and met everyone she could. Lois explained, "Starting as an entrepreneur in a small company, I did every trade show. And where a lot of companies didn't find trade shows a very good return on investment, they were the best investment we made. It was because we used them differently. We used them to meet everyone. I would go and meet people, not just customers, but I would get to know everyone in every other booth. I'd learn what they do, why they made certain decisions, and who their buyers were. And by getting to know people, and by being open, I built a network of people who referred customers or great employees to us. And the sales reps on a trade show floor become sales managers, CEOs, and executives. And by then, they were our friends. My network grew up with me as they also moved up the ranks and moved around in different companies."

Lois followed this principle: get out there and connect. Meet everyone. Tell everyone. Listen. Her approach created a network and community of people interested in Aquire's business.

Talking to everyone and engaging the right people, in person or through social media, creates early interest, but it can also make your wave feel inevitable. Joe Nussbaum, who created The Big Event at Texas A&M, described his approach to these conversations: "I told so many people about it that the idea became legitimate in a very short amount of time."

MAKE IT EASY TO SAY YES

Allen Stephenson started Southern Tide as a 22-year-old college student after spending a semester abroad in Italy. In Florence, he saw fashion dramatically different in look and quality from what he knew at home. When he returned to South Carolina, the American fashion he had worn growing up felt fresh and new. Even though he was a biology major with plans to attend medical school, Allen regularly took his polo shirts apart and reconstructed them so they would fit just right. He began to connect the quality and construction of clothing he had seen in Italy to the American style he had always known. He initially desired a better polo shirt that looked, fit, and felt better.

When Allen first began, he created prototypes. He went to M. Dumas & Sons, a premier clothing store in Charleston, South Carolina, carrying his prototype shirts in a Gap bag—nothing was even branded yet.

Allen said, "I asked to talk to the store manager and said, 'I have these shirts I'd like to show you.' He told me that the last thing he needed was another polo shirt. I said, 'I know—you're right. I'm not trying to sell you polo shirts.' He was confused and wasn't clear where I was going. I said, 'I'm going to give you these. I made them, and I'm really impressed with them, and I want to see if you are, too—or if your customers are. Here are a dozen shirts in different colors and sizes. Just take them. Here's my number. Just give me a call if you get a chance, and let me know what you think.'"

After a few weeks, Allen got a phone call from the M. Dumas & Sons manager. The manager said that not only did they want to order some shirts, but they were also interested in creating a small wall to feature them. Allen said, "And that was it. That was when I knew it was happening."

Allen's wave started because he did his homework first, making it easy for his target store to say yes. He even gave a few shirts away at first so the employees and customers at M. Dumas could try them. He let the product speak for itself.

> **We moderated ourselves. We didn't ask for the world.**
>
> —Fiona Grant

When Bob Wright started the bigBANG! event for the DSVP, they began by inviting a few people to meet and talk about their plans. They didn't ask them to commit to being in a group, to join DSVP, or to sign up for a year-long community service committee. They asked, "Will you come and talk about our idea?" That was it. And it was enough.

> **Communicate with clarity and conviction. Share what's in it for them. Confused people walk away.**
>
> —Tory Johnson

DON'T EXPECT CONSENSUS

Of course, no group of people will agree on everything. When you set out to build your wave, this is important to remember. Assume you will face disinterest, resistance, and naysayers. Lack of agreement isn't the same as resistance.

When it comes to change, consensus isn't the goal. Know where you need support, where you'd prefer it, and where it doesn't matter. I recently had a colleague tell me with disappointment that her ideas were shot down. After some questions, I learned she had one meeting where she'd fielded some tough questions. She received some interest, but not across the board. Based on that discussion, she decided the time wasn't right. Her expectations were probably unrealistic. Most new ideas will face skepticism. It isn't a reason to give up so soon.

Clint Hurdle, former Manager of the Pittsburgh Pirates, said the word "conflict" has a negative connotation, even though it's essential. He said, "Conflict or tension is really important in honest communication. As an example, if a base runner makes what looks like a poor decision, you have to confront it—but do it in the right way. The first thing I do is ask the question, 'Tell me what you saw out there,' and I listen to the answer. Then, the next day, we look at the tapes together and match that up to what he saw at the time. This is a chance to learn. And it's a lot more effective than yelling at a player, 'That it was a stupid play,' in front of the team as he enters the dugout. He knows he made a mistake. Constructive confrontation is how we learn and understand each other."

Rather than use a lack of consensus as a setback, learn from it and decide if you can move on without it. Mark Benton, currently a VP of HR at McKesson and who previously redefined careers in R&D at PepsiCo, explains how he balances listening and respect with persistence: "You have to have to have a deep respect for people. We all want to be heard. If I give others the respect and the dignity of hearing them out, then I feel like they need to give the same to me. Then, hopefully, we can all come to an agreement that will accomplish something, but you won't get everything. And, ideally, we'll find some common area to agree or compromise."

> **We don't have to agree; we just need to understand each other. If we understand each other, there's potential for us to get something done.**
>
> **—Mark Benton**

Most Wave Makers do not expect complete consensus but understand that many waves need sponsorship to make progress. In studying Wave Makers, I found that they use strategies to keep them moving forward even without consensus. They:

- Use individual collaborative conversations more than group "selling."
- Listen to understand another point of view, even if they disagree.
- Ask for early input from key people so it is considered and included upfront.
- Accept that some people won't be on board, treat them respectfully, and find a path to move forward. In my interviews and client experiences, I've learned that many initial naysayers became supporters after some success, so the initial lack of support can change over time.
- Take small but deliberate steps rather than going for that one big formal decision that could shut the effort down before it is fully understood.

Every organization is different. But, in any situation, you must keep the naysayers in perspective.

Keep the need for approval or agreement in perspective. Paul Zellner, a former senior executive at Russell Reynolds, has been a friend and advisor for many years. He spoke to our company about growing relationships and clients, as Paul is an expert in this area. One of his points has stuck with me. He talked about the importance of embracing "Oh well." He said he has learned that you can't take a lack of interest personally and assume you'll never make progress. He reminded us that everyone has their own priorities and agenda, which may not fit yours. Of course, you learn from every interaction, but sometimes you just say, "Oh well. I tried to build a relationship," or "I tried to introduce a new idea, and it didn't work that time." It doesn't mean it never will or that you made a mistake. Learn from it and carry on. You don't need everyone's approval to reach your goal.

THINK TIME

1. What opportunity do you see that no one is asking for today?
2. What values are undeniable in your organization or community?
3. What values do individuals in your organization or community believe in?
4. Who cares about the same issues that you care about?
5. What gaps in knowledge do you have that others can address for you?
6. Who are three to five people to be in your Idea Circle?
7. What opportunities do you have, or can you create informal conversations to develop ideas or options?
8. What simple goals can you share with others?
9. How can you prepare to involve others without developing the answer in isolation?
10. What resistance can you expect, and how can you plan for it?

NOTES

1 Dan Roam, *The Back of the Napkin: Solving Problems and Selling Ideas with Pictures* (Boston, MA: Portfolio, 2013).
2 B.J. Hogg, *Tiny Habits* (New York, NY: Harvest, 2021).
3 Dan Roam, *The Back of the Napkin: Solving Problems and Selling Ideas with Pictures* (Portfolio, 2013).
4 Alan Siegel and Irene Etzkorn, *Simple: Conquering the Crisis of Complexity* (Twelve, 2013).

5

Planning a Wave That Lasts

You've started. You are past the most challenging part—deciding to begin. You've addressed your fear of taking action, you have the idea that matters to you and others, and informally created your Idea Circle. Now, it's time to build on your momentum and start a lasting change.

You're ready to experiment, plan, and build sustainable interest. Most planned changes never make the leap from great ideas to reality. Research says only three out of seven change initiatives succeed, or 70% fail. We can debate the exact number, but it's clear that many intended changes never come to fruition. In this chapter, we'll look at how to plan and organize your wave so it lasts.

> **Ideas are a dime a dozen. It's all about execution.**
>
> —**Tory Johnson**

Yet, we can't project manage every step in a change even though many change models imply otherwise. Change isn't controlled by any one person in any organization. Changes have a life of their own.

As Mike Morrison, Ph.D., and Clint Kofford share in *Creating Meaningful Change*, "Most of us assume that we can effectively manage our change efforts as rational, step-by-step process...We get into project management mode as we clarify our overall change goals and the milestones to get there. In other words, we believe we have more control than we actually do. This false assumption, more than anything, contributes to the high failure of change initiatives. While any change effort will benefit from a project management mindset, true transformational change

78DOI: 10.4324/9781032715339-8

is more about people than managing them…Change in organizations is influenced by just about everyone and controlled by no one."[1]

Any successful change has a roadmap and implementation plan. Yet, plan to adapt along the way as you learn more. You'll need a flexible plan, as you haven't done it this way before. Much like the human wave at a ballpark or a rock thrown into a pond, the ripples of a change continue well beyond the starting point. How far you can see will affect your plan.

> MYTH: You have to make a plan and stick to it.
> REALITY: You transform your life by starting small and being flexible.
>
> —BJ Hogg[2]

We love to talk about our goals! We write goals down, put them on the wall, and often stop there. Research finds that over 40% of us have given up on our New Year's resolutions by the end of January. We want to run a marathon, start a business, get promoted, or change careers. Goals are very important—but our success requires connecting goals to action and what we can control. What steps can we take to move us closer to starting the new business or running five miles? Motivation and dreaming fuel us to get started but won't carry us past a few weeks.

Nick Saban, the former head football coach of Alabama University, recently retired as a winner of seven national championships and one of the most successful college coaches in history. Saban coached his players not to focus on the outcome—winning the game, becoming the SEC champion, or taking home the national championship. Instead, he expected them to focus on "the process." Or, in other words, their contribution to every single play, practice, and their daily work. He expected his players to ignore the scoreboard and stay singularly focused on doing their job at the highest level or what was in their control on each play and every single day. He said if you do that, the wins will follow.

James Clear, author of *Atomic Habits*, agrees. He said, "Achieving a goal only changes your life for the moment. That's the counterintuitive thing about improvement. We think we need to change our results, but the results are not the problem. What we really need to change are the systems that cause those results. When you solve problems at the results level, you only solve them temporarily. In order to improve for good, you need to solve problems at the systems level. Fix the inputs and the outputs will fix themselves."[3]

> You never start by talking about the results you want on the field. It's about how the players talk and think. They need to take ownership of the game and the team. When that happens, the results will take care of themselves.
>
> —Clint Hurdle

THINK BIG, PLAN SHORT

Ask yourself these key questions before you develop the next phase of your plan:

- What is my desired impact? How will I know when it is realized?
  - Sense of purpose
  - Financial
  - Service
  - Engagement
  - Other relevant metrics (quantitative and qualitative)
- How have my goals changed based on input from others or learning more
- What is my "process" for change? What are the daily habits I can change?
- What can I do? What is in my control?
- Where do I need others?
  - Support
  - Sponsorship
  - Resources
  - Knowledge
    - Who isn't involved but should be?
    - If anything stops my wave, what will it be?

Let's plan your wave. As discussed in the previous chapter, planning too much detail too far in advance can work against you. Most waves are unpredictable and hold surprises, so stay flexible and be prepared to adjust.

Of course, large-scale changes need key milestones and a thoughtful plan, yet ensure you don't let your desire to plan affect your adaptability.

Plans are created with assumptions that will undoubtedly change over time. We can become very attached to a plan once it's agreed upon and in place. I was in a discussion recently when the team realized that their original plan was based on old, outdated assumptions. Since the plan had been hatched, conditions had changed, and the company had new faces with new expectations. The environment had changed, but the team and their plan hadn't. They subconsciously viewed changing their plan as a mistake or failure.

You may remember Wave Maker Brooke Averick from Chapter 5, the well-known social media podcast host, TikToker, and comedy creator. She thought preschool education was the obvious choice for her career, but not what she really wanted to do. After she started reading from her old diaries on TikTok during the pandemic, her impact grew, and she now hosts two successful podcasts and creates other content. She couldn't envision her dream was even possible at first, so her action plan was always very short term. And, she said knowing what she *didn't* want led to realizing her goal. If she had relied only on her goals at that time, she would have missed the bigger opportunity.

Brooke shared, "When I started making videos on TikTok, I viewed it as something that'd eventually get me a good job closer to what I wanted to do. Maybe I could be a journalist at BuzzFeed, I could write articles, or it would bring me to a better office job. I never thought it would bring me to what I'm doing now and being self-employed. But, I never closed my mind to the possibilities. In the beginning, I saw sharing content as a stepping stone to getting to a better job. I just never imagined that I could be doing what I'm doing now."

You're never done with change. It's not episodic. It's continuous.

—**Mark Benton**

YOU ARE HERE

Google Maps has a blue dot that shows you where you are. Your starting point will determine your route and how long it will take to get there. You need to know the same about your wave from two perspectives:

How big is the change for you? and How significant is the change for others in your family, team, organization, or community? The gap will impact your plan and possibly your timing.

Let's begin with your starting point. How big is this wave for you? How big is the gap between where you are today and where you want to be? Like Brooke, can you even envision all of the possibilities now?

Big goals can seem impossible at first. The goal to lose 50 pounds, participate in your first 10K, and start a company when you've always worked at a big company can feel too big and, as a result, keep you stuck. Yet, if you start with what you can do today that is entirely in your control—you have step one in your plan. Look for smaller "chunks" or phases you can plan out in the short term.

Trust the process while you also take in new information, see what is around you, and look for a new door to open.

A friend of mine started a complete health overhaul for herself and her family. She began by setting a goal to run a 10K race in one year. She had a big gap from her starting point because she was pretty inactive, but she gave herself enough time and set incremental goals each day. By the third month, she was running short distances, and the family menu was much healthier. She also learned that having a running partner really helped her, especially on cold, rainy mornings, so she and a neighbor joined forces in month three. She got there step by step.

Emma Scheffler, the Wave Maker who started Insulin Angels as a high school student, knew nothing about starting a nonprofit but had an idea and a passion. She had to rely on others to help set up her organization and make it a reality. The gap didn't keep her from deciding to act.

Also, consider the starting point of your organization or community. How big is the change for everyone involved? How will that affect your approach and timing?

Fiona Grant, an HR leader at Accenture at the time, knew she was taking on a significant change when she and her team set out to convince senior leadership to introduce domestic partner benefits. Fiona saw the broader commitment to diversity and a CEO who spoke of bold change, yet it was a very established global management consulting firm. Fiona worked closely with others who cared about this issue. They developed a thorough business case based on facts and extensive research. Given the magnitude of the change, she understood that it would take a comprehensive and well-thought-out recommendation with the facts to back it up. She knew her starting point and developed her plan accordingly.

THINK TIME

1. What is your starting point? Where are you today?
2. How dramatic is the change you want to pursue?
3. Does your group or organization feel the need for your change, or do you have to create the need?
4. How equipped are you to pursue this change?
5. What knowledge, information, or partnerships do you need based on where you are today?
6. What is step one in your plan? What can you do today?
7. How far ahead can you see?

BE AN INCREMENTALIST

A change takes a plan but not a rigid project plan. Keep your destination in clear focus as you develop your approach—much like the route on a map. You plot and adjust your route as you learn more about conditions and needs.

Think about a football coach who has his team prepared with a game plan to exploit the other team's defensive coverage. But on game day, the coach realizes their opponent made major adjustments and has changed their prior defensive schemes. The coach must make quick game-time adjustments and experiment in real-time to see what works to win the game. Be ready to make incremental changes and often "just in time."

In a Hollywood Reporter roundtable, producer Margot Robbie described how she approached the Mattel executives to gain their support for making Barbie, the highest-grossing movie of 2023. She brought them along the change curve and they eventually approved a movie that didn't always portray Mattel in the best light. She said, "The strategy was 'Let's all get very comfortable being uncomfortable'…just get it to the next stage, and before you know it, we'll be on the set. Greta (Gerwig, Barbie director) said, 'Drive it like you stole it.'"[4]

Her message was step by step—but keep moving.

> **The plane was moving, and we were absolutely building it while we were in flight.**
>
> —Mark Benton

The best plans for a wave are incremental—reacting to new and changing conditions—yet aimed toward the big goal. Incremental planning is:

- Future focused even if it's short term
- Continually learning and incorporating new information
- Adaptive and flexible
- Short horizon, with clear long-term goals
- Collaborative
- Take what you can get

Incremental planning assumes you make those adjustments as you go and still reach your goals—even if your goals change over time. Some Wave Makers, like Brooke Averick, started their wave and not only made notable changes along the way but also changed their goal because the potential became much more significant than they'd ever imagined.

> **We were incrementalists. We knew our goal, but we got there step by step.**
>
> —Fiona Grant

James Clear points out the impact of small changes every day in Atomic Habits, "The impact created by a change in your habits is similar to the effect of shifting the route of an airplane by just a few degrees...If a pilot leaving from LAX adjusts the heading just 3.5 degrees, you will land in Washington, DC, instead of New York. Such a small change is barely noticeable at takeoff—but when magnified across the entire US—you end up hundreds of miles apart. Similarly, a slight change in your daily habits can guide your life to a very different destination. Making a choice that is one percent better or one percent worse seems insignificant at the moment, but over the span of these moments that make up a lifetime, these choices determine the difference between who you are and who you could be."[5]

Here are tips for finding the right balance between no plan and too much structure:

- **Have clear goals**, even if you decide to adjust them over time. Keep your goals simple and know your direction.
- **Stay flexible** so your decisions are actionable, but be ready to adjust as you've not done this before. A change to the plan isn't a mistake; it's expected. You may not be changing your destination, just how you get there. Be open to the idea that your goals may evolve and become much bigger than you ever imagined.
- **Keep asking, "What are we learning?"** The most essential topic in any planning conversation starts with: "What do we know now that we didn't know before? Given what we have learned, what adjustments are needed?"
- **Remember the human side of planning**, not just the deliverables and actions. Guwan Jones preferred individual conversations with important contributors because she felt they were essential in learning what needed to change, not just to sell her ideas. Know who's impacted and whose input is needed and keep returning to your "why."

I reserve the right to get smarter.

—Mark Benton

MOVE WITHOUT A PERFECT SOLUTION

Earlier in this book, we talked about perfectionist paralysis—the mindset that says, "I can't begin until it's perfect!" Decide when 80% is good enough to get started.

> **I've found that my gut instinct is a lot more reliable when I've assimilated lots of information.**
>
> —Lois Melbourne

Lori Meyers, a Wave Maker who heads up Chase's Place, became president of this unique school for children with developmental disabilities. She explained that, at first, she just didn't know enough to do everything at 100%. Her comment has stuck with me. Lori said, "I finally decided that my 60 percent could make all the difference, and it was enough. I just kept going." Your 60% may be enough to make notable progress, not because you don't want to give 100%, but because 60% is all you know how to do or that time allows.

Also, some waves are part of more extensive changes, so the assumptions constantly change. If you wait for the perfect solution, the parameters will change by the time you begin implementing it.

An adaptable and flexible planning approach allows you to adjust your plan over time and aim for your 80%—and maybe eventually reach your goal. As a new entrepreneur, I learned so much so quickly that I gave 150%, but my contribution was about 60% because there was so much I didn't know. By staying flexible, I compensated and adjusted as I learned more rather than sticking with my original plan or definition of success.

Bob Wright, Wave Maker and creator of the bigBANG! community event in Dallas, said, "We tried to be inclusive from the outset. We never tried to openly own the idea. We went into meetings with our partners and coconspirators with about 80 percent of what we wanted. We allowed them to mold the other 20 percent and I think they felt like they owned 50 percent. It became community owned before it became community questioned."

I've always loved the Lorne Michael quote to Tina Fey in *Bossypants*. Fey shared that she was often still improving the Saturday Night Live skit until time ran out. She said Michaels had to always remind her that "The show doesn't go on because it's ready; it goes on because it's 11:30."[6] There are times when the deadline arrives whether we are ready or not.

Think about it: What would it be if you had to make one move? Decide how you can begin to make progress now. The first step is almost always the hardest.

Wave Maker Lindsay Pender spent six years as a neonatal ICU nurse at one of the top metropolitan hospitals in Philadelphia before moving to a much smaller town and hospital. She believed that what she had learned previously would be valuable to this smaller hospital, which didn't have access to the resources and technology of the city hospital.

Her first step was to ask other nurses and respiratory therapists if they felt specific practices in the pediatric ICU nursery were working. She also talked to a more senior leader about ideas she felt would help the babies in the ICU, and she received a receptive response. She then joined a task force that focused on improving processes and procedures. She was thoughtful about her first steps and made progress while recognizing that she couldn't make these changes alone. She knew she wanted to start a change but didn't want to be the "know it all or put anyone down." Lindsay didn't look for the perfect solution, yet she was patient and found a way to get started and make progress.

> I knew I wanted to start a change. I just found what I thought was the best way to get started.
>
> —Lindsay Pender

EXPERIMENT WITH A DEADLINE

Because waves are new, they require experimentation and likely some failures. Remember that a wave is different from a project or initiative. It's an exploration.

In *The Creative Act: a Way of Being*, legendary music producer Rick Rubin, shares the importance of experimentation. He said, "There's no right way to experiment. Generally speaking, we want to begin interacting with the 'seeds', developing our starting point in different directions... This is one of the fun parts of the project because nothing is at stake. You get to get to play with the forms and see what takes shape... In the

Experimentation phase, conclusions are stumbled upon. They surprise or challenge us more often than they fulfill our expectations."[7]

It will take some experimentation and testing to see what works and what doesn't—but you need a deadline.

An experiment is defined as a test, trial, or tentative procedure to discover something unknown or test a principle or supposition. Experimentation must be timely and quickly serve as input for your plan. It isn't a reason to lose ground or delay as you continue testing and looking for the perfect answer. Unless you are in a research role that requires a predefined time frame for testing, you should use testing to confirm that your change is sound, try your boldest ideas, get others involved in the experiment, and learn before you share more broadly. But remember that timeliness and speed are usually essential elements in creating and sustaining momentum in any change.

Sim Sitkin of Duke University uses the term "intelligent failures" to describe experimentation and how we learn from trying and testing. Sitkin's criteria for intelligent failures are:

- They are planned so that when things go wrong, you know why.
- They are genuinely uncertain, so the outcome cannot be known beforehand.
- They are modest in scale so that a catastrophe does not result.
- They are managed quickly so that not too much time elapses between outcome and interpretation.
- Something about what is learned is familiar enough to inform other parts of the business.[8]

These criteria are meant for learning, quick interpretation, and action. Notice the key words "test," "trial," and "tentative." An experiment is not the same as an early release or pilot. The purpose is to learn and adjust.

> **When you experiment and lead a fundamental change, there will be lots of mistakes. Learn and keep going.**
>
> —Melisa Miller

Waves require testing and experimentation because the ideas are new and often haven't been done before. Almost every Wave Maker I spoke with used experimentation and found it to be fundamental in both learning how to make it work and creating momentum.

Your experiment may involve sharing product ideas with potential customers, asking one hospital to test a new process for patient admissions, or trying a new recruiting experience in one division. Decide what you need your experiment to do—the questions to answer and the assumptions to test.

Experiments in one environment can be viewed as mistakes in another. Melisa Miller, Advisor to and former President of Alliance Data emphasized, "I told everyone that we are going to make a load of mistakes because we are trying too many new things not to." She took on a multiyear change to reward risk and experimentation, representing a vast culture change. She made experimentation safe by communicating that it is valued and that mistakes are expected. Mistakes through experimentation are learning mistakes.

Be bold in your experimentation: step out a little. It's an experiment, after all, and you'll have time to adjust. This is the time to try your boldest ideas—you can pull back before you activate more broadly if you need to.

Lois Melbourne, co-founder and former CEO of Aquire, shared how she thinks about risk, "Take the risk you can stomach. Know your limitations upfront and whether you can handle the worst-case scenario or most likely failure—and if you think you could recover from it. Then, once you've thought that through, go do it."

FIND YOUR EARLY WINS

Remember, the definition of a wave is a transfer of energy that creates momentum. A critical way of starting momentum is through early visible successes. In sports, teams like to score first to create an inevitability mindset in their opponent and to build team confidence. The same is true in your wave.

In business, "quick wins" are important, whether leading a big change from the top of the organization, starting a new business, or starting a wave in your community. Momentum builders are your wave's first impressions. Early wins also help keep you motivated as you see progress toward your goal. Almost all Wave Makers I researched relied on momentum builders or some variation of quick wins for their waves. Early successes will buy you time.

Jonathan Morris, previous Chairman of North Texas YPO and current CEO of Titan Bank, shared the importance of early wins. He said, "Get some initial successes. Go after some quick wins to validate your plans. And, even if it doesn't turn the naysayers around, it will buy you enough time to move forward and put in place what is needed. And the naysayers may just come around when it works."

Fiona Grant, a Wave Maker who led the creation of domestic partner benefits at Accenture, had a surprising early win for her cause. It was a baby shower. Fiona shared the personal side of her story. Fiona said, "The big thing was that Heidi, my partner, became pregnant with our baby-to-be, Daisy. And she's a schoolteacher. But she decided that she was going to stay home. So, I had a situation looming that was a personal need for me. I had to be sure they could both be on my insurance. I had to adopt Daisy, and that was complicated in itself. But I couldn't add Heidi to my health insurance because there was no policy in place for domestic partner benefits."

She explained that a baby shower turned out to be a turning point in her journey. Fiona said, "The office threw me this fabulous baby shower, and everyone was just so incredibly welcoming and supportive of me being like them, a parent. Everyone wanted to talk about baby stuff." She said she had every reason to believe that Accenture would be supportive because of the personal support she had received from so many.

She explained that the domestic benefits topic became personal not just for her but for others too. Fiona said, "It was a huge eye-opener and a major normalizer. I'd been used to looking in from the outside. And becoming a parent suddenly did two things. One, it gave me normalized access to the rest of the world, which was empowering in itself. And secondly, I was now advocating not just for myself but on behalf of my family. And as a woman, that puts things in a different light. The shower was a turning point." One event started the needed momentum.

MOMENTUM BUILDERS

Identify your momentum builders for your change. Also, watch out for some potential traps. Make sure your momentum builders:

- Are strategically aimed toward your bigger goal
- Aren't a distraction at the expense of higher priorities
- Are one step toward longer-term progress
- Are real and will be viewed as momentum builders in a few months, not just today

Momentum builders aren't all alike. It's essential to consider the type that will be meaningful and helpful to your wave. The momentum builders you need in one situation may go unnoticed in another. Momentum builders may include:

Quantitative results. This may be a noticeable improvement in sales for your new store or product. It can be an uptick in participation, increased attendance at your events, or a noticeable cost decrease. These momentum builders are quantifiable and hard to debate. Some in your community will need this quantifiable result to take notice.

Melisa Miller, Advisor and former President of Alliance Data Services, said that an immediate improvement in financial results was a momentum builder. Still, she had to manage the good news. She said, "We hit our first financial goal very quickly. It started happening so fast that I had to ensure everyone remembered that we still had much more to do."

Confidence builders. Confidence builders matter early in the project as it gives you and others confidence in the change. When starting a project with a new client, we always discuss 'first impression work.' This goes beyond the first meeting or conversations to how can we quickly deliver on a commitment. You build confidence in a fantastic first set of first deliverables. This gives the client confidence that you can lead a client through their change effort based on that first but critical phase of work.

Positive word of mouth. As discussed in Chapter 3, positive word of mouth and personal recommendations are the best ways to build momentum for anything, including your wave. Positive buzz about the new change helps—whether it's the new company, a new working location, or creative virtual working.

Inevitability. Inevitability is based on quick progress communicating that your idea and plans will be successful—so why not join in?

Joe Nussbaum, creator of The Big Event at Texas A&M, said his team built momentum by talking to so many people that their idea became legitimate in a very short amount of time. Their momentum builders consisted of multiple actions and conversations but resulted in a feeling of inevitability.

Some momentum builders are a surprise, but many can be addressed in planning or even created. I have been part of many large organizational changes designed around a few momentum builders. This gave the effort a positive first impression that helped build momentum.

Let's face it, you don't have long.

—Joe Nussbaum

THINK TIME

1. What is your natural planning style? Will it help you or get in the way? What adjustments will you need to make?
2. What will you design for your "process" based on small actions to a bigger goal?
3. How big is your change? How much will that affect your planning?
4. How can you realize incremental progress—even if small at first? Are there any natural phases for how you approach your change?
5. What is the best way to incorporate a flexible planning approach?
6. What experiments will help you see what works?
7. What ideas do you have for early wins? Where do you need them most?
8. What momentum builders will help you keep your change going?

NOTES

1 Mike Morrison and Clint Kofford, *Creating Meaningful Change* (Venice, FL: Archangel Ink, 2022), p. 41.
2 B.J. Hogg, *Tiny Habits* (Boston, MA: Harvest, 2021).

3 James Clear, *Atomic Habits* (New York: Penguin Random House, 2018), pp. 17–18, 25.

4 *Hollywood Reporter Roundtable*, Rebecca Keegan, January 4, 2024.

5 James Clear, *Atomic Habits* (New York: Penguin Random House, 2018), pp. 17–18, 25.

6 Tina Fey, *Bossypants* (New York: Little, Brown & Co., 2011).

7 Rick Rubin, *The Creative Act: A Way of Being* (New York: Penguin Random House, 2023), pp. 150–151.

8 Sim Sitkin, "Learning Through Failure: The Strategy of Small Losses," *Research in Organizational Behavior* Vol. 14 (1992): 231–266.

6

Creating a Community around Your Change

Now that your change is taking shape—it's time to expand your circle to build more support and interest. And, with a community around you, progress doesn't depend solely on you!

"Community" describes those who care about what you care about and show it through action. A community is a group actively committed to the cause. It's made up of people who care, want the outcome you want, and contribute. Communities aren't created based on a job title, position, or an organization chart. They are built around a common cause.

Before you think, "I could never create interest around one of my ideas," let's take another look. Here are examples of Wave Maker created "communities" that propelled a wave:

- Those who supported a new local charity that eased the fears of children diagnosed with diabetes
- An informal working group dedicated to improving the delivery of client projects
- A neighborhood Bible study that met the needs of moms learning to navigate children going to college
- A group of parents with a passion for expanding the fine arts curriculum in their school district
- A women's networking group dedicated to mentoring, learning, and sharing
- A new business venture built on support and belief from others

DOI: 10.4324/9781032715339-9

Wave Maker Gretchen Seay, co-founder and Managing Director of Clearsight Advisors, shared how she built interest in their company when they launched in 2011—in the middle of the financial crisis. She said, "I've always had a mindset of being a connector so that $1+1=4$. When I met people, I always thought about how to be helpful, whether or not there was a business opportunity. I naturally think about the longer relationship. So, when we started the business, I just got out there and met as many people as I could. I knew I had to build a circle of people who could vouch for me and us."

This circle of supporters continued to advocate for her and Clearsight as they grew and expanded the business. Gretchen built her community by helping others accomplish their goals while growing their new business.

She added, "I've always made having a great network a priority. And I especially wanted to help other women and create situations where we could help each other."

Here are the key ingredients for a successful community that will propel your wave forward:

1. Clear purpose & change that matter
2. People who care
3. People who share

PURPOSE & CHANGE THAT MATTERS

Any lasting change is based on a purpose bigger than one person; it's a change that makes the community, work, family, or marketplace better. A bigger purpose will keep you going when you have setbacks and disappointments—and you will. What you do next is what matters. And, if the purpose matters more than the setback—you'll keep going.

We have discussed the importance of finding true meaning throughout *Make Waves*. A community must be dedicated to something bigger to stand the test of time—an issue that matters today and will matter tomorrow.

The Wave Makers I've met and worked with built their changes on values, a purpose, a dream, and meaning that brought others to their cause. Their stories begin with a diverse mix of important causes, from a culture change to starting a new business and being a champion of diversity. But the causes were all bigger than just one person.

> **When you focus on the much bigger prize no one complains about the coffee anymore.**
>
> —Rich Sheridan

More about Us and Less about Me

The classic rule of sales and influencing is to help your audience see "What's in it for me?" This principle is generally true, but in the extreme, it can place too much emphasis on self. Waves are different. You aren't looking for the quick yes so that your target will buy a product or approve the request. You want to rely on purpose.

"What's in it for me?" may help others get on board at first because they know it will give them something they value (more money, better hours, more support), but interest will fade over time. In a change, go one step beyond to "What's in it for us?"—as a community, organization, family, or world. If you remember to think about what's in it for us, you get to more significant values and purpose with sustainability that will engage others.

> **If you focus on "What's in it for me," you promote individual agendas and priorities. Go for the purpose that isn't dependent upon the extrinsic rewards.**
>
> —Rich Sheridan

When Rich Sheridan redefined how teams created software at Menlo Innovations, he changed almost everything. Rich said, "I reminded them why they chose this profession of developer to begin with. Sure, at the most basic level, it's typing into a computer. But we chose this career to make something better. Over time, in organizations, people can lose that sense of purpose, and they seek extrinsic rewards to balance it out. We had to return to our purpose of why we were doing this work to begin with and find the joy in it again."

PEOPLE WHO CARE

A change needs people who care about the cause and are committed to making it a reality. When people join forces in effort and ideas, the impact is enormous. Caring also has to translate into action. The classic question in this book is, "What can I do?" Once there is a belief in the purpose, the cause, or the outcome, the question of "What can I do?" will come naturally.

Encourage Accountability

Accountable, caring people are essential in any change because caring translates into commitment. Accountable people ask, "What can I do?" and "How can I help?" They spend their energies on what's in their circle of influence. Even if you have a small working group interested in getting your idea off the ground, you will need accountable participants ready to roll their sleeves up and help. Leading or contributing to any change requires getting into the arena and taking on some responsibility.

Promote Collective Ownership

Collective ownership doesn't mean a free-for-all or no accountability, but rather that community members are partners, not recipients. Everyone contributes sometimes and receives at other times, but everyone has a role to play. Communities may have a leader or organizer, but it isn't a command-and-control, hierarchical structure. All members think of themselves as "owners" and contributors. I love how Bob Wright of Dallas Social Venture Partners described people involved as almost like parents of the change.

> When we finished, we had a hundred mothers and fathers of the bigBANG!
>
> —Bob Wright

The idea that we are all contributors is essential to our economy. You can share your apartment, car, or office by the day. A sharing community shares what they have, usually at some profit, and everyone benefits. A community is a similar concept. It shares the assets and solves problems together.

Wave Maker Trisha Rae is the founder and executive director of Christmas is for Children. One of the organization's big events is the annual food basket assembly on the next-to-last Saturday before Christmas. The room bustles with energy and Christmas carols while hundreds of families and students enthusiastically load thousands of holiday baskets for the community. At my first event, the baskets were bursting with food and ready to go by noon, as planned. It was a big success.

Afterward, I mentioned to Trisha that I saw a few opportunities to make this fantastic event more efficient and streamlined. Tricia said something that stuck with me, "Yes, we probably could make it more efficient, but people like to feel like they are part of it and have some choice in what they work on. So, if we are still finishing on time, a little bit of overlap or inefficiency may be okay."

As someone who studies and advises on organizational change and behavior, I paused because she was so right! How did I miss it? When we were meeting the objective, the trade-off for more efficiency had more downsides than benefits in this situation. She and the team created an event that built commitment for the event and the cause. This organization is successful because so many people are invested in the Christmas is for Children community and the event—not as spectators but as contributing participants.

I remember that story when I think of collective ownership because optimum efficiency may come at the expense of letting others have a voice and a hands-on role. And the community that stays committed can do so much more than any single process change.

Collaborate with Intent

A community works together to solve problems, realize goals, or make something better. It has a purpose. You can't be a spectator. Collective ownership means many voices, not just one. And it means that everyone contributes—there are no spectators.

I facilitated a leadership workshop recently, and we played word association with the word "collaboration." The leaders in the room mentioned these words more than once:

- Slow
- Groupthink
- Lacks focus
- Inefficient

This group associated collaboration with wandering meetings, fruitless brainstorming sessions, and input with no outcomes. If it's a basic task, a process, or a crisis, "collaboration" may live up to all these words. After this session, I decided that "collaboration" might need a PR campaign.

Collaboration is more than asking everyone for their ideas. Productive collaboration needs a well-thought-out process and a purpose that is transparent to everyone. It doesn't happen by bringing a group together and asking them to join hands and collaborate. It is very intentional, with a desired outcome. Collaboration takes time, a process, simple tools, encouragement, and guidance.

Ask for input and collaboration on areas where you need it, not on predetermined or nonnegotiable outcomes. Recently, a client asked their leaders questions about if they should collaborate more with other divisions to sell their services. Yet, their business strategy and financial goals already required this collaboration. Their clients had given feedback that this financial services company was confusing to work with because of multiple contacts and being too siloed. The right question would have been how to make collaboration work across divisions and share client relationships—rather than if they thought it was important or not. The company's leadership had already made that decision in their multi-year strategy. Ask for input from where you need it.

In many of the Wave Maker stories, they used collaboration to move their wave forward, even if progress initially seemed slower. While collaboration may seem inefficient in the beginning, if used properly, it can accelerate momentum and build momentum.

Demonstrate Mutual Respect

A strong, vibrant community values the participation and involvement of all members. This respect must extend to everyone involved in the community regardless of role, experience, or interest. A community is not a hierarchical group but one where all can participate. The most powerful aren't the decision-makers in communities. Likewise, all members have a responsibility to speak up and participate.

> **You develop trust through complete transparency.**
>
> —Clint Hurdle

Trisha Rae of Christmas is for Children explained the importance of respecting everyone's talents and contributions, and especially valuing volunteers. She said, "Find the strengths of the people who want to help. Some volunteers can't see their gifts and their talents. But help them see them and find where they can contribute and be part of making it all happen. It's important for you, your goals and them too."

Use the Magic of the Small Group

Commitment is more likely when we know our participation is needed. When you attend an event with more than 30 people, have you noticed that it's easy to be a spectator rather than an active participant? Because the group is big enough, you can step safely to the sidelines, smile, nod, and leave. It's officially someone else's responsibility. But your silence is noticed if you are in a discussion with less than ten people. And it's easier to pull everyone into the conversation. The size and scale need to be considered when you define your community.

A few years ago, when Julie Porter, CEO and founder of Front Porch Marketing, was in the early days of starting her business, she used the small group concept perfectly. She invited a diverse group of people she knew and trusted over to her house for dinner with the "ask" of giving her advice and ideas for starting her new business. Over wine and dinner, there were new introductions, and people caught up after too long. One guest helped another with a job connection, and others discussed new business opportunities. Julie had pillows on the ground and flip charts in the corner of her living room. One friend acted as the facilitator. A few key questions were posed to the group on defining the company name, brand, and target market. We all left that night with new or renewed business friendships. Julie had a great list of ideas for her new venture and, best of all, had created an ad hoc community of people behind her business. She also started a great word of mouth based on who was involved and how it was created. It all began with a small, informal group.

If your wave is extensive and, as a result, the community is big, remember the small group. Even if your wave is smaller, your small group may be your community and the engine behind your momentum.

PEOPLE WHO SHARE

A community grows by people committed enough to share the importance and value of the change.

When We Care, We Share

Your wave must have purpose and relevance for others to care. As Richard Millington shares in *Build Your Community*, "The secret to a thriving community is *relevance*. Think about how many people are fighting for your attention right now... The war for your attention is ferocious. So, why would they decide to participate in your community? If you can't answer this question, your community is doomed. Your audience will only visit and participate in your community if it is the most relevant method for them to satisfy their needs and desires..."[1]

Sharing takes effort and time, and there are many competing demands for our attention. Know why people will care about your idea and how it helps. We discussed the importance of building your wave on values and what matters most. Connect these values to your stories and conversations.

Jonah Berger, author of *Contagious: Why Things Catch On*, says, "Naturally contagious content usually evokes some sort of emotion .... Emotional things often get shared. So, rather than harping on function, we need to focus on feelings."[2] Our feelings are tied to meaning, which we know is essential in any wave. If we do this, what will be different or better?

You'll remember that we talked about the value of inevitability. One of the ways to realize inevitability is if your wave is not only needed and essential but will solve future problems. It's current and relevant. We all want to believe we are part of improving the future. If your change delivers on that promise, make that connection for everyone involved.

Many Wave Makers used informal, individual conversations to discuss their ideas. This strategy has many benefits, including showing you care about both their participation and the cause—because both matter. I have found a significantly different result when I ask colleagues for their input and involvement via a group email or in a big meeting versus when I ask one-on-one. It's much easier to care when two people have a real conversation. This connection can be a critical element at the beginning in making your wave contagious.

What does your wave need to become contagious? If you are starting a podcast that you hope will grow your business, you need to know what your audience cares about and how they can engage. Let's say you want other parents to support more funding for the arts in your school. The first step is deciding how to gain commitment from a small core group so interest can then spread to other parents. If you plan to turn a business around, you must balance your metrics with visible outcomes others care about and want. If you are starting a new business, consider what will make your future customers care about your plans.

Lois Melbourne, Wave Maker and co-creator and former CEO of Aquire described how her company engaged its customers in new and unexpected ways in the beginning: "We were working out of the house, and yet people from all over the world were downloading the software and testing it with a thirty-day trial. At that point in time, no one was giving away enterprise software. We were bucking the system. So, people were testing it, trusted it, and bought it because it worked. It built a network because people trusted the software and, as a result, they learned to trust us."

At that time, Lois and her team found a new way to engage its customers and community by sharing its software, and that openness created a personal connection and great word of mouth.

Connect the Vision to Real-Life

We've learned that translating concepts into real-life stories creates engagement and personal interest. Information becomes relevant and meaningful when we picture and experience it. There are countless articles and books on storytelling, and most speakers and writers use stories to engage the listener or reader. Storytelling can translate strategies, analytics, and metrics into real-life relevance. It is also essential in a wave. An illustration brings "the why" to life and accelerates commitment. It also helps your wave spread.

At a United Way event, they shared their important work supporting the education and training to help 18-year-old foster children successfully enter the workforce. They had a thorough presentation including data on their impressive results. Yet, the room's interest level completely changed when we moved from the overview of the services and programs to a single speaker. This young woman slowly and hesitantly walked to the front of the room. You could see she was nervous speaking to this large group. But she movingly told her story and how this program had given her a chance to start over, learn a skill, and progress to a supervisor at her company. The story of the real-life impact is how United Way built the support and commitment from this group to get involved.

Guwan Jones, the previous leader of Diversity & Inclusion at Baylor, Scott & White, was so insightful in sharing the impact of diversity on patient care. I asked her if they committed to plans that would have a real-life impact. Guwan said: "If we have culturally diverse health educators, then they can influence the entire team. For example, if the physician, who isn't from the patient's culture, works with a health educator and understands some of the barriers for the patient, it can be considered upfront. So, the physician now understands that the closest pharmacy for this patient takes three bus trips. And can we give her a ninety-day supply of medication? And if finances are a big concern, let's look at the $4 drug list at Walmart and try to find an option there. We'll also look at the communication. All of the paperwork is in Spanish, yes, but it may be university, formal Spanish, and it's confusing to the patient. If healthcare providers understand the barriers, it can change how they interact with patients. Then it's no longer that the patient is non-compliant; it just needs to be translated to their world and situation."

After Guwan's simple, real-life stories, I understood that diversity in patient care isn't a corporate program; it is about direct patient care—her passion.

Painting a picture plays a vital role in your wave because when you communicate your plans, it's essential to describe the vision in a way that connects to others and the bigger goal. However, storytelling is a communications strategy, not an outcome in itself.

I watched a CEO talk repeatedly about the importance of giving examples and sharing stories his audience would connect with. And he was pretty good at it—in front of the room. He could tell stories, but the problem was that it was a performance. He didn't have the same ability to connect when he wasn't on the stage, so he couldn't translate his excellent speaking skills into action or commitment.

Like this CEO, a dazzling performance isn't enough. As we've discussed throughout *Make Waves*, the conversation and collaboration are where your wave gains traction. Telling meaningful stories is essential in one-on-one conversations, as in my discussion with Guwan Jones, not only in big meetings.

> **Tell stories and make it real but have your facts and be informed too.**
>
> —**Fiona Grant**

With the caveat that storytelling isn't just a dazzling performance but stories can be helpful to:

Inspire for the Future

A few years ago, I contributed to planning an organization-wide change that affected almost everything and everyone—new processes, technology, roles, and ways of interacting with customers. Our strategy was to describe the new world after the changes occurred. We used examples and real-life situations to convey that the short-term pain would be worth it because tomorrow would be much better for everyone. They had to get a glimpse of a better tomorrow before seeing the potential—and understand the short-term pain would be worth it.

Lori Myers, Wave Maker and president of Chase's Place, said that one of her first actions in her new role as school president was to build more communications support: "We needed financial contributors, but we also needed people who contributed with their hands and their time. I had to find ways for others to see the good we were doing in this school. We used videos, visits, and personal stories to help others see what we saw."

> **Most people deep down want to help others and children in our community. I knew that if anyone walked into this school, met these children, and heard their stories, they would be committed to Chase's Place.**
>
> —**Lori Myers**

Straight Talk

Straight talk is simple and authentic. We previously discussed the importance of simplicity in purpose and goal. Simplicity is critical to building interest in your wave and growing the community because it makes your change easily understood and the goals clear. In business, we can get sidetracked with overengineered language designed to impress more than engage and help others understand.

I like to use the "neighbor test." You have more work to do if your neighbor can't understand your change. Your neighbor is a great example because she is not involved in your work and may not completely understand what you do. And that is exactly why she is the perfect test case. Your message must be simple, clear, and compelling, even to your neighbor.

Sometimes, our fears, discussed in Chapter 2, reappear when we share our ideas. Those fears that cause us to wonder, "Am I smart enough?" or "Are my ideas important enough?" can translate into using "important" language designed to make us sound and feel significant. This fear can cause simplicity to take a backseat to complexity.

For a long time, I've loved the book *Why Business People Speak Like Idiots* by Brian Fugere, Chelsea Hardaway, and Jon Warshawsky. It is a laugh-out-loud look at how business communication is drowning in jargon, acronyms, and buzzwords, along with some great ideas for how to fix it. The authors say, "The average professional goes to the office every morning and plugs into e-mail, checks their voice mail, and walks into meetings only to be deluged by hype and corporate speak:

> After extensive analysis of the economic factors and trends facing our industry, we have concluded that a restructuring is essential to maintaining competitive position. A task force has been assembled to review the issues and opportunities, and they will report back with a work plan for implementing the mission-critical changes necessary to transform our company into a more agile, customer-focused enterprise."[3]

This example would be hilarious if it weren't so true. If you work in a large organization, there is a good chance you live this every day. Some businesspeople use this jargon as naturally as they use technology. As a Wave Maker, fight the urge to join in. Remember that your goal is to find meaning and connection. Corporate speak will only undermine you.

A few years ago, I had a very compelling and honest conversation with a leader before an important meeting. He then excused himself to speak to his team in front of the large hotel ballroom. Suddenly, everything changed. How did this natural, engaging human being turn into the corporate actor in front of the room? He relied on the "business speak" he had learned over many years and missed making a connection to the employees in the room. It comes from years of wearing a work mask and an unconscious belief that this is what you are supposed to do. But it doesn't have to be that way.

Fugere, Hardaway, and Warshawsky identify four traps that keep us from communicating in real language: obscurity, anonymity, hard-sell, and tedium. I want to mention the hard-sell trap now because when you start a wave, you are trying to influence and convince—not use the hard-sell. They say: "At the end of the day, people hate to be sold to, but they love to buy. With access to loads of information and instant communication, people today question everything. They know the hard sell and—with trust in business at an all-time low—even the slightest whiff of it sends people running for the exits."[4]

Where do you draw that line? Be positive and share the opportunity, but don't hide the challenges. The "shove it under the rug" strategy means that problems will reappear later with more power. In a wave, you want to create momentum builders for your change, but totally unexpected problems can derail your progress. You are much better off being open about the risks, likely problems, and predicted bumps in the change. This realistic view of the change helps you and your circle expect and manage through the adversity that you know will be there.

I was involved in an acquisition when the most senior leader stood in front of the new employees and confidently said there would be very few changes. "Just think of this as business as usual!" he said. The newly acquired employees were so relieved and pleased with this exciting news.

Yet, given the rationale for the acquisition and the agreed-upon business plan, there was no chance of that happening. As the weeks unfolded, more and more significant changes were introduced. This leader bruised his credibility and trust with this group so badly that he never recovered. In his first communication, he had gone for what he thought was the easy, comfortable answer, and, as a result, he wildly overpromised. The employees learned drip by drip that he wasn't telling them the truth.

Wave Maker Melisa Miller, Advisor and previous President and CEO, made many changes in her wave as head of the retail division, but not to her ultimate objectives. Her instinct was to be open, lay it all out, and then get moving. She knew that if she kept her communication simple and direct, the 3,000–plus employees involved in the change would understand the change and their role in it.

> **I'm a big believer in pulling the Band-Aid off at once and starting to move forward.**
>
> —**Melisa Miller**

Everyone's wave is unique and different, yet all depend upon simple and honest communication to maintain the integrity of both the Wave Maker and the wave.

Meet Others Where They Are

As you start sharing your ideas and plans with a broader group, it's easy to assume that everyone knows what you know. After all, you have been thinking about this topic for months or years. Now, it's time to go back to the beginning and remember that this broader group is new to your ideas. Newcomers need time to absorb and catch up. And, not everyone will want to get involved in the same way.

At PeopleResults, "meeting our clients where they are" has always been a frequent conversation. Often, the ideal solution just isn't viable for a client. They may have a limited bandwidth for the change, no budget to take on a more extensive program, or may not see the need. Or, more likely, their starting point is such that they aren't ready for the ideal strategy or have the right tools to pull it off. The company may need a comprehensive change program to support its focus on cybersecurity, yet step one is starting education and communicating essential information to key audiences right now. Meet them where they are—not where you think they could be or should be.

Lindsay Pender, a neonatal nurse, shared that she was driven to help seriously ill newborns by what she had learned at her previous job at a metropolitan state-of-the-art hospital. At the same time, she knew that her fellow nurses at the new, smaller hospital needed time to absorb this new information and hear her perspective. She recognized that she was at a different starting point in her smaller hospital, so she was patient and open to others while maintaining her commitment to the desired change.

When you are five steps ahead of your broader community, remember that you are much further down the change curve than everyone else. You are planning the change when the others are way back at, "Why are we doing this???" Being this far out in front of others may be challenging if you like quick action and are ready to go. Instead, reset to what your community needs to know—not what you already know. Meet them where they are.

Mark Benton, a VP of HR at McKesson and previously redefined careers in R&D at PepsiCo, shared how he adjusted his pace to stay in sync with others: "I had lots of ideas and plans, but I didn't bring out all my ideas at once. That was a big learning from one of my senior leaders. I had all these wonderful things I wanted to do and deliver them all at once. I got smart advice to pace myself and not try to do everything at once."

> **Understand that not everyone may have the same appetite for change that you do.**
>
> —Melisa Miller

Combine Enthusiasm and Substance

The truth is no one will ever be more enthused about your ideas than you are. You set the baseline. Enthusiasm doesn't mean you need to be energetic, perky, fake, or spin. You don't need to command the room. Enthusiasm simply means you have confidence and believe in the direction and goal.

In my experience studying change and wave makers, I have found this to be true repeatedly. Everyone shows enthusiasm in their unique way. Some have excitement in their voices when they share their experiences, while others are quieter but exude confidence and belief in their change. They are all very different people pursuing different changes, but each brings their unique brand of enthusiasm and authenticity.

Substance and knowledge are the other ingredients to go with enthusiasm. As Thomas Queen, Partner at Queen, Sands, & Schutz, a successful legal firm, shared, you need substance and knowledge first before you can bring others along with you. He said, "There really aren't any shortcuts. There is a process I know backward, forward, and sideways for M&A (mergers and acquisitions)—the technical side of any transaction. It's really only once you have that down that then you can start to freestyle and figure out how to simplify it and share with others."

Show enthusiasm in a way that is comfortable for you. Be yourself. Be authentic.

— **Julie Porter**

THINK TIME

1. What is the cause that matters in your wave?
2. How can you ensure that your wave is focuses on "What's in it for us?" rather than just "What's in it for me?"
3. How can you promote collective ownership?
4. What strategies can you use to promote accountability?
5. What is your natural communication style, and will you have to adjust to ensure you don't assume too much?
6. How can you connect real-life stories to your larger purpose?
7. How can you improve your ability to connect with others?

NOTES

1 Richard Millington, *Build Your Community* (Upper Saddle River, NJ: Pearson Educated, 2021), Chapter 2.
2 Jonah Berger, *Contagious: Why Things Catch On* (New York: Simon & Schuster, 2013), p. 23.
3 Brian Fugere, Chelsea Hardaway, and Jon Warshawky, *Why Business People Speak Like Idiots: A Bullfighter's Guide* (New York: Free Press, 2005), p. 1.
4 Brian Fugere, Chelsea Hardaway, and Jon Warshawky, *Why Business People Speak Like Idiots: A Bullfighter's Guide* (New York: Free Press, 2005), p. 1.

7

When the Wave Comes to You

Waves can start with your great idea or a surprise request from your manager. Significant changes may appear out of nowhere, and you have no choice but to take them on. Personally, there are many of these life changes—the loss of someone you love, a job elimination, the diagnosis you never anticipated, a job offer in a new city, or a new assignment at work when you don't feel ready. Surprising, unplanned changes may bring sadness or joy, but none of these changes were in your plan and can really test your adaptability.

In these examples, your change began because it arrived unexpectedly. You had no choice. Yet, you'll decide how to keep going and move forward.

Let's look at two types of waves that you didn't plan:

1. Leading through an unplanned wave that arrives unexpectedly
2. Contributing to a bigger wave that affects you, yet someone else designed

LEADING THROUGH AN UNPLANNED WAVE

Wave Maker Lori Myers is president of Chase's Place School. The school was founded because nearby public and private schools weren't meeting the needs of children with disabilities. But being the president of Chase's Place School was never part of Lori's master plan. She explained, "Another couple started Chase's Place School in 2003, and we started my daughter there when she was just 5 years old. And then, in 2010, the school owners decided they could no longer continue for many reasons. They met with a

DOI: 10.4324/9781032715339-10

group of parents and told us they planned to leave." As we processed their decision, the next question was, "Would you guys like to take over? The parents that day ultimately said, 'Yes, we've got to do this.' So, we talked it over and decided we just had to figure it out. There really weren't any other options. There was no way we could realistically find the right place for our children in just a few months. So, we decided to put our heads together and keep this going."

Lori described how she organically became a Wave Maker: It began when she realized how much this school mattered to her and her family, so she was "all in" for helping the group. And then, somehow, she became president of the board. Lori didn't look for the wave. It came to her. Lori explained, "I have this bad habit of taking over. I can't mind my own business. And I really didn't mean to do this because I had young children, one with special needs. And my initial reaction was, 'How in the world am I going to manage this? I'm busy!' I don't have a lot of idle time. Yet, my fear was, 'How are we going actually to keep this going?' I feel like I'm good at finding good people, knowing what deficits I have, and where we need to find experts. We now have the right experts and team in place. And I tried to put some business parameters in place. Cut costs and focus on the structure and the right priorities. I did everything I could to make our vision stay alive."

In this example, Lori's change wasn't her idea, and at first, she hesitated. Even when a wave isn't our idea, like Lori, we can ask, "What can I do?" and "How can I help?" Especially when it was apparent someone needed to step in to reach the ultimate goal. She decided it was her.

Neena Newberry, CEO & Founder of Newberry Solutions and award-winning business leader, shared her very personal story about the change that came to her. She said, "On January 2nd of 2020, I was diagnosed with breast cancer. Of course, that was a very surprising start to my year. So, when we talk about dealing with change—step one for me was just to cry my eyes out for a day. And then get the emotions out of my system. Then, I picked myself back up and said, 'Okay, let me step back and really think about this and where I'm at.'"

Neena explained, "A big part of it for me is being very focused on what I know versus what I don't know. I got to a place of putting everything into perspective and saying, wow, cancer is a scary word. And, the treatment was a lot more complicated than I thought it would be at first. I had to ask, 'What is it that you know? What is it that you don't know?' And be really mindful about where I put my energy. And my feelings evolved. I'll just fast forward to kind of the end of my story with breast cancer, that thankfully it's gone."

Two key differences exist between the wave you envision and the wave that appears in front of you: (1) how and why it starts and (2) your level of control or influence.

Like Neena, when the wave comes to you, you must first internally absorb and process what the change means. The more significant the personal impact—the more thought work it will take from you. Educate yourself on the new situation. Then, eventually, decide your options. Options can clearly define what you control or influence. Ask yourself, "Even if I didn't choose this change, what are my options and choices?"

I quickly learned I had to focus on the here and now.

—Neena Newberry

Options

I find identifying your options is the most practical method for getting your mind right and making wise decisions. Looking at options can clarify a hard decision and help you know what to do. The path that initially seemed undesirable might look very different compared to other choices. Considering all options is a very valuable and insightful exercise for making any significant decision.

Start by listing your options with no prescreening or prequalification. Include every option, including what initially seems stupid or a bad choice, as one bad idea may spur a new idea. List them all. And remember to include the often-forgotten option of doing nothing.

We are often fooled by the pretend safety of not making a decision. Yet, not deciding is a decision. It's deciding you are comfortable keeping things just as they are—at least for now. Yet, while no decision may feel like the lowest risk or safest—this option may have significant consequences. You may miss your window for returning to get your degree, receiving medical attention early enough, or not pursuing the job opening at your dream company that never opens up again. Don't put "doing nothing" in a separate category, as it is an option and a decision with consequences too.

I recently had a significant experience looking closely at the "no decision" option. The company I founded was recently acquired. Our company had grown and expanded into a larger organization with global clients, dozens of projects, bigger teams, and more complex work. We reached a crossroads where we had to decide, "What do we do next?" The goal was to ensure the business was sustainable and continued forward not only for our team but for our longstanding clients.

After taking a step back and looking at all options, I soon realized, along with my other partners, that we needed more investment and support to continue scaling and growing the business. We had reached a tipping point. We looked carefully at all our options: (1) do nothing and keep going but make some tough decisions internally, (2) find investors and likely have key decision makers not involved in the ongoing success of the business, or (3) look at being acquired by the right organization. While we played out multiple scenarios simultaneously, we knew the tradeoffs and pros and cons by assessing and contrasting each option. The acquisition option by the right company was ultimately our best path to reach our goals for the team and our clients. Yet, when we started the exploration, doing nothing seemed to be the simplest option—until it wasn't.

Sharing the options considered is also a great way to help others understand why a hard decision was made. The best example I've ever seen is watching the CEO of a Fortune 50 global products company speak to about 200 professionals who were very frustrated about planned benefit changes. This company was known for offering great benefits, but benefit costs were skyrocketing, and rules were changing. The buzz in the organization was not good. You could feel the tension when the CEO walked to the front of the packed room.

The CEO spoke to the audience like the adults they are, with complete transparency and confidence. She explained each option considered and the impact of each one. Most importantly, she shared why executive leadership landed on this decision. The CEO articulated clearly that the decision was made with care and thoroughness. And, rather than using her position to push or defend the decision, she was transparent that while the outcome wasn't perfect, it was the best of the options. You could see the mood shift in the room as they understood that while they didn't love the outcome—they now understood the rationale for the choice and preferred it to the other options. They understood "the why."

Exploring all options helps most decision-making, especially when it's a wave you didn't choose because you can contrast and compare the choices rather than looking at one path in isolation. You may not have chosen this change, but you do control how you react to it.

When the wave comes to you, there are a few key questions to ask yourself—after looking at your options:

- How can I best reach my goals or the best outcome in this situation?
- What thoughts or emotions may get in my way and need my attention?
- What will I need to learn or change?
- What can I do now to move forward?

How Can I Reach My Goals in This Situation?

Understanding your starting point is essential when reacting to an unplanned wave that comes your way. Learn everything you can about this new situation through research and talking to experts. This assessment is critical so you know how to reach your goals even if you aren't in control. Understand what you need to learn or change to move forward. Before you commit to the outcome, understand your starting point.

A friend we'll call Jenny wanted to start her own public relations business within five years. A trusted colleague approached her—a successful business owner in her field who planned to retire, and he suggested Jenny buy his business. Jenny was thrilled that her entrepreneurship dream was on her doorstep. Even though it was a little earlier than planned, she loved that she wouldn't have to start from scratch. Her excitement built as she pictured herself hopping on the fast track to owning a full-scale PR business.

At her mentor's urging, Jenny asked an independent expert to conduct a thorough business assessment. She soon learned that the business's profit had trended downward over the past three years and that one client represented over half of the company's revenue because of a close relationship with the current owner. At first, it seemed like a once-in-a-lifetime opportunity. But, after pausing and looking at the facts more closely, Jenny reluctantly concluded the business wasn't a wise investment for her. She was better off starting her business from the ground up. But, if she hadn't taken the time for a full assessment, she might have acted too soon just because the opportunity appeared in front of her.

Earlier in my career, I was asked to take on a leadership role in building our global services business at Accenture, a significant change in strategy for our organization. I found the work content very interesting, and I was enthusiastic about the new challenge. However, at the time, our two boys, Will and Patrick, were young, and I was limited in how much travel, especially global travel, I was willing to do. So, right up front, I shared my personal boundaries and let my leadership know that if I took on the role, I'd have to carefully manage and control my travel. I was clear that I would have to do the role my way for it to work. They agreed. And that was the main reason I agreed to move into the role. It was my way of deciding, 'What can I do now to reach my goals in this situation?' while fully knowing it may mean losing the opportunity.

What Do I Need to Learn or Do Differently?

As we've discussed, any change requires taking in new information, building new skills, and newly formed insights. This situation often requires even more attention to learning because the change wasn't anticipated. It is critical to ask these questions:

- What do I need to learn that I don't already know today?
- What's my timeline for educating myself in this situation?
- What knowledge do I need that I can't obtain myself? What other experts do I need?
- How will I get the needed expertise? What is my learning plan so I gain insights and information from others?

I've found that educating myself on anything new is one of the best ways to reach acceptance, define options, and see my first steps. It's common to miss making time for education, especially when this change wasn't part of your master plan. We love to already know the answers rather than admit we have a lot to learn. This can be due to our ego or feeling too busy. Yet, if you bring the same toolkit you brought to a similar situation five years ago—there is a high likelihood you won't know what you need to know now. In my research, Wave Makers were consistently ready to learn and had an unflappable belief of "I'll figure this out."

Mark Benton, Wave Maker, a Vice President of HR at McKesson and former Senior Director at PepsiCo, was asked to develop and activate the first global strategy and plan for growing careers in PepsiCo Research and Development—a big and complex request.

> **I knew I'd be successful and that I could do it. I just didn't know how yet.**
>
> —Mark Benton

Mark knew this high-profile request had high expectations and opportunities too. His first step was to make sure he understood the problem to solve. Mark said, "I listened and gathered information. Given the high expectations, I knew I had to move quickly. So, I relied on some of what had worked well in other groups and brought my new ideas that fit R&D. I created an important core group of people who were there with me and became ambassadors for the change."

Mark quickly sized up the situation by asking, "What will it take?" and he used creativity and a practical approach to make progress. He also realized that he had to tackle this global change in phases. He couldn't wait until everything was complete before introducing the completed R&D career model and new program. Speed mattered. It also helped his team learn while they simultaneously started moving toward progress.

Mark said, "One of my biggest lessons was the importance of phasing and pacing, not just for me and my team but for the organization. There was a limit to what could be absorbed at one time, yet I needed to move quickly. Don't wait to reveal everything at once."

Also, in times of personal crisis, such as a divorce or surprise medical report—seek out the information you need to make the right decision. A friend just started the first steps toward getting a divorce. While it was painful and hard, she said getting information helped her know what to do next and what mattered to her. Meetings with her financial advisor, attorney, and real estate agent were difficult. Yet, soon, she felt more informed and finally ready to take the first step in moving forward with her new life. Educating herself and gathering more information gave her the peace of mind to make important decisions.

What Can I Do Now to Move Forward?

When a wave comes to you, it can be harder to answer, "What can I do now?" You may not have started with a passion for the idea, or it may have arrived when you weren't ready. While we have repeatedly discussed the importance of the first step, this lack of control can make it even harder to have confidence at first.

Neena Newberry shared that on hard, unplanned changes, it can be hard to know where to begin. She said, "When you are facing anything big or overwhelming, personally or professionally, you don't have to figure out the whole thing. You don't have to solve it all. Just think about the next one or two steps you need to take and how can you do those well." Rather than take on the entire situation or problem, break it into smaller and manageable pieces. Throughout *Make Waves*, we've discussed the importance of those first small steps that lead to big changes.

One of my favorite quotes is from *The Boy, the Mole, the Fox, and the Horse*,[1] about a boy who couldn't see his way out of the forest and didn't know what to do.

> The boy says to the horse, "I can't see my way forward."
> THE HORSE: Can you see your next step?
> THE BOY: Yes.
> THE HORSE: Then take that step.
> After taking that one step, the boy looks at the horse and says: Now what?
> THEHORSE: Can you see another step?
> THE BOY: Yes.
> THE HORSE: Then take that.[2]

The horse offered great wisdom in asking, "Can you see your next step?" Like Neena Newberry or Mark Benton, they both focused on the first step and then the next one in two very different situations. But, for today, the first step was enough.

> **You can't be that kid standing at the top of the waterslide, overthinking it. You have to go down the chute.**
>
> —Tina Fey,
> *Bossypants*[3]

THINK TIME

- What is needed to reach your goals—even if you didn't choose this wave?
- What options are in front of you?
- How does the wave match your passions, values, and interests?
- What must you learn?
- What role can you play in the success? What unique gifts do you bring?
- How can you work with others to reach your goal?
- What is your first step? How can you move forward now?

CONTRIBUTING TO A BIGGER WAVE

We all contribute to changes around us that we didn't originate at work, in our communities, schools, or families. This role as a contributor can be as important as starting or leading a change. Anyone who starts a change needs you. Even Wave Makers can also wear an important contributor hat.

It can be challenging if you didn't choose it and are just contributing to someone else's change or idea—it can feel easier to sit back and not get involved. And, in these situations, it's more natural to think, "I would have done it differently." This is a common reaction but not a reason to stay on the sidelines.

Being a Critic Keeps You Stuck on the Sidelines

Being a critic isn't a high-level skill! It's pretty easy to point out everything wrong. Critics also know this is a very effective tactic for keeping the responsibility squarely on someone else's shoulders. This point has never been made more eloquently than one of my all-time favorite quotes by former President Theodore Roosevelt:

It is not the critic who counts; not the man who points out how the strong man stumbles, or where the doer of deeds could have done them better. The credit belongs to the man who is actually in the arena, whose face is marred by dust and sweat and blood; who strives valiantly; who errs, who comes short again and again, because there is no effort without error and shortcoming; but who does actually strive to do the deeds; who knows great enthusiasms, the great devotions; who spends himself in a worthy cause; who at the best knows in the end the triumph of high achievement, and who at the worst, if he fails, at least fails while daring greatly, so that his place shall never be with those cold and timid souls who neither know victory nor defeat.

This quote is also a reminder that we will be judged or criticized when we lead or do anything significant. Online comments and critiques of successful music artists, actors, or entertainment personalities are brutal. The bigger your impact, the more likely you'll hear criticism—especially if you change how it's always been done. So, if you are "in the arena" and accountable, you will be noticed by the critic. It's the law of human nature, so plan on it.

I've always used this important accountability coaching point for those on my team with aspirations of taking on a bigger role. You must be more than someone who points out problems: you need ideas and recommendations for solving, changing, or innovating. One of my favorite leaders at Accenture, Don Monaco, always listened to our problems and concerns and then always asked, "So, what's your recommendation? What do you think we should do?" I learned very early that if you see problems, you must also do your research and bring recommendations or at least options. Admiring problems keeps you and your career right where you are.

Critics can wield power, especially over those lacking confidence in themselves or their ideas. If you want to be a valued contributor or trusted leader, leave this full-time critic mindset behind unless you review movies or restaurants. This doesn't mean you don't see the problem—you do— but assess it and consider the options. We can stay stuck admiring the problem when presented with an uncomfortable change or a change we wouldn't have chosen. Participate and look for solutions. Keep your focus on "How can I contribute?"

And, as a change leader, upgrade your listening skills because even the critics or naysayers have valuable information for you. Listen and consider input without feeling threatened. Treat feedback as potentially useful information, as you want to know what could go wrong. But that doesn't mean it keeps you from moving forward or taking input or criticism personally.

> **Criticism is something you can avoid easily—by saying nothing, doing nothing, and being nothing.**
>
> **—adapted from Elbert Hubbard**

Know What You Bring to the Party

The ideal is when your interests and abilities match the needs of the new change. It's essential to decide when and how you are best equipped to contribute. I previously hired someone for my team with the perfect expertise and outstanding client relationship skills. But there was one problem: he had to contribute to and influence multiple organizational changes, and he didn't understand the culture or the business well enough yet. He was too new and had limited knowledge of our industry. So, my first step was to identify a key team member to be his guide and help with his blind spots. He knew he had a gap, but we developed a practical plan to address it.

Lori Myers, Wave Maker and president of Chase's Place School, shared that she had no choice but to depend on others. She had business and organizational skills but needed others to balance her limited educational and marketing expertise. She knew what she brought to the party, and those skills were essential in preparing her to be successful. She also knew what she didn't bring—which was just as important.

Contributing to a bigger wave in your work can be as simple as asking yourself and your team, "What does this change mean for us?" and "How can we incorporate this change into our work?" My company was recently acquired by a larger company with different services and ways of working. We had to learn to combine the businesses and always return to "What does this new way mean for us?". This led to a list of actions and changes we wanted to make.

One of my clients is committed to creating a safety culture beyond just safety policies and metrics. Their philosophy is to take care of each other and help everyone get home safely to their families at night. Everyone knew how to bring care and concern for the team to all their decisions, even if they were new. For example, one of their employees keeps a picture of his grandson on his phone as a reminder of the importance of safety. He won't forget.

Start a Ripple

We have mentioned the power of ripple effects throughout *Make Waves*. These begin with small decisions and actions within your control that propel a larger change. Go for even small things to give the bigger wave momentum.

Here are a few examples of people making small decisions that started a ripple and contributed to the bigger goals of the organization or community:

- The manager who regularly calls and texts her team members to check in during challenging organizational changes.
- The product developer who changes the development process to involve customer discussion groups much earlier as part of the company's strategy to be more customer-centric.
- The R&D scientist for a food and beverage company who has regular informal lunches with the nutrition team leader to encourage communication and coordination, given their strategy of developing more nutritious options.
- Neena Newberry, the business leader who faced a cancer diagnosis and yet decided that while she is a very private person, sharing her story was her best way to help others in the same situation.
- My mother-in-law, Helen Johnson, who became an active volunteer at the Alzheimer's Association after she faced the grief of her husband's diagnosis.

Find small changes you can make today to contribute to the bigger goal. Remember to ask, "What can I do now?" and "What can I influence or control?" You can make a significant contribution even when the wave comes to you or you are part of a more significant change you didn't start.

THINK TIME

- What can you do to move beyond problems and find ideas for moving forward?
- What do you need to learn to better contribute to the change in your organization?
- What are the needs for making the overall change successful?
- What unique talents do you have that can help make the change happen?
- How can you incorporate the new change into your day job and daily activities?
- What actions can you take that will start even small ripples and help bring about more significant change in your organization or community?

NOTES

1 Charlie Mackesy, *The Boy, the Mole, the Fox and the Horse* (San Francisco, CA: HarperOne, 2019).
2 Charlie Mackesy, *The Boy, the Mole, the Fox and the Horse* (San Francisco, CA: HarperOne, 2019).
3 Tina Fey, *Bossypants* (New York, NY: Reagan Arthur Books, 2011).

8

When Your Wave Hits a Wall

Not every wave will work. Some will never get started or reach the result you intended. For all the success stories, I also heard: "I couldn't get others interested," "It was a great idea, but there was no funding," or "Despite my best efforts, I couldn't get my business off of the ground." Every Wave Maker has setbacks and problems. Yet, they instinctively knew setbacks were a natural part of change.

We all have failures and disappointments. Every one of us. This discomfort is how we learn, grow, and get better. Reframe how you think about a setback or disappointment. Anytime you take on a new opportunity or face a challenge like nothing before, it won't be a straight line on progress. A setback or disappointment at first can become something you learn from and keep going if you change how you think about it.

As Brene Brown has shared in many of her interviews, "There is no innovation or creativity without failure. Period." George Clooney, successful actor, director, and producer, had this to say about failure, "You learn nothing from success. You really don't. You learn everything from failure, everything. And how you handle it is important, and what you take away from it is even more important."[1]

If we all listed the times in our lives when we learned the most, we'd undoubtedly have failures and difficult times high on our list. Your job was eliminated, the interview for your dream job didn't go well, the relationship that didn't work, or the business you tried to start never worked. We wouldn't have chosen these outcomes, but we learned something and became stronger. And that is the point—truly learn from your experience *first* before deciding what to do next.

There is no one-size-fits-all answer. There's no foolproof advice as simple as "Be persistent and keep going!" Likewise, a setback isn't a reason to say,

DOI: 10.4324/9781032715339-11

"I'm done." At times like this, become a scientist and objectively assess why you hit a roadblock. Gather information and be open to where it leads you. Learn from your setback by doing an unbiased analysis before you decide on your next step, much less give up.

Cynthia Young, a Wave Maker and leader who changed the culture at her organization said, "You have to be willing to make room for the possibility that you missed something. It doesn't mean your overall plan or what you're trying to accomplish is wrong. It just means that you might have to change tactics, not strategy. Not everything is going to have your ideal neat, happy ending."

> **You are going to hear no. Expect it and keep going.**
>
> —Trisha Rae

First, determine if you've actually hit a real brick wall or just a setback. As I researched those who started waves, I realized that one of their distinguishing factors is a willingness to size up obstacles, adjust, and work through them. To keep going. As discussed in Chapter 2, Wave Makers' that focus on impact rather than personal recognition makes the setbacks less significant or personal. And, their adaptable persistence comes into play here.

In this chapter, we'll explore how to assess if you have just a setback or a wall and the wisdom to know the difference. Each roadblock is different, so look closely at your unique situation for new insights. I also think this type of assessment is valuable for any setback you experience that involves others.

YOUR DIAGNOSIS

A diagnostic is a method for identifying the nature and cause of any condition so you can draw conclusions. After your doctor conducts tests, you may be diagnosed with strep throat. A personal trainer assesses your muscle strength before creating a customized workout plan. It's a way to assess the facts and rule out other options. Now, it's time to turn that analysis on ourselves.

While it may be challenging, lift up and look at your situation objectively with no assumptions or bias. Step away from your personal feelings, disappointment, and judgment. Use whatever metaphor works for you: reporter, scientist, or business analyst. Pretend you aren't involved in the situation and only look at the facts. Ask yourself, "How do you know?" Make sure your answer is based on data and information—not your speculation or feelings about the future. Seek input and perspective from others, too, as it can be challenging to assess why something didn't work as you had hoped completely on your own. Have you noticed how it's much easier for us to see and solve others' problems than our own? Use this phenomenon to your advantage!

A few years ago, I led a global change initiative. A key executive sponsor changed the expectations, timing, and expected outcome at the last minute. I understood her reasoning, but this new direction was a game-changer. I left feeling defeated, disappointed, and frustrated. My team was in disbelief and a little angry as we discussed the change, which came after months of work and just weeks before a widely communicated launch date. I told them we'd all take one night to be frustrated. But the next morning, we'd have to put all our energies into how we'd adjust our plan given our new direction. We had to leave our frustrations behind so we had a clear head for deciding our best option for moving forward. We ultimately decided to simplify and scale back our plan to meet the deadline while maintaining quality. This was a setback—not a wall.

After setting aside your frustrations or disappointment, objectively analyze why your wave didn't go as planned.

Assess the Situation

Consider these questions as you begin your assessment.

1. *What was your original objective?* Recall the original intent when you envisioned your wave. Return to the vision and revisit why you believed it was important.
2. *What were your actual results?* Consider what actually happened, not how you felt about the result. Focus on facts. What was happening

when you made progress and, likewise, when you hit the roadblock? Like a scientist, look at each step, what happened, and the timeline.

3. *What feedback did you receive from others on your idea?* What was the feedback? Who gave it to you and how? How relevant was the feedback? We know you can't expect consensus on a new idea or wave, but the feedback you receive is vital to consider in your assessment.

   It's essential to dive into the specifics of the feedback you received. Was input different for the idea than the implementation? Who provided the input, as well as how and when, may affect the relevance. Were your naysayers professional naysayers who poke holes in any new idea from anyone? Did they have a personal bias that runs counter to your change? For example, suppose you had resistance from someone who values efficiency above all else. In that case, he may not support taking time for experimentation, even if it is valuable in the long run.

   Some waves require agreement from your leadership in advance. If you didn't get support or agreement, review the factors that affected that decision—timing, viability, cost, or need. Consider this information objectively before deciding, "It didn't work."

> **You should listen to as many people as possible. But if someone tells you, "You shouldn't do that," you shouldn't just stop. Because people will.**
>
> **—Allen Stephenson**

4. *What was your progress, even if you didn't realize ultimate success?* Have you noticed that when we discuss lessons learned, we love to go straight to the problems? If, like me, you could have a glowing performance review but leave only thinking only about the area for "growth," it's time to change your habits. It's easy to find missteps, such as "I didn't explain my idea well enough in that key meeting," "I didn't have a good enough prototype," or "I should have tested it more before I got leadership involved." All these obstacles are important and may be true—but what worked well?

I've had many experiences when my idea/plan/change didn't gain traction initially, yet I knew I was building support for next time. Recently, a client wanted to introduce a company-wide change in performance and talent development all at once. I encouraged him to break the change into mini phases so leaders understood it first and could successfully implement it in their teams. He resisted at first, but I knew he heard me. As we continued to work on the design and implementation plan, others gave him similar feedback that it was too much to introduce at once and expect success. We eventually came up with a variation that moved quickly but in short burst phases that worked in his and the organization's best interests. We got there because we listened, adjusted, and stayed true to the principle of "how can this change be successful?"

5. *What didn't work as you had hoped?* Identify the disappointments or breakdowns that you haven't already considered. Think about the forces that worked against you, no matter how small. Examples might be:
   - The expected sponsor who stayed on the sidelines
   - The big kickoff event that had to be rescheduled, which hurt the momentum
   - The meeting where it became evident that not all costs had been considered
   - The failed pilot program that created an initial lack of confidence in the product
   - The interview for the dream job that just didn't go well

6. *What made your wave stop?* Summarize in one or two sentences what made your wave hit a wall. Know the simple answer to this question, then dissect and see what you can learn. This isn't about how you feel; it's about what happened.
   - If your funding was canceled, why was it canceled? Was it because of the viability of your project or other unrelated business issues?
   - Was your request for funding out of synch with the annual budgeting cycle, so you were too late to get investment approval?
   - If a critical sponsor wasn't on board, why? Was it the concept or how it was presented? Or did they not have the bandwidth to get involved at that time?

- If your new business didn't reach your first-quarter minimum goal, was your target realistic? What progress was made in that quarter that may impact the next one? What obstacles need to be addressed?
- If you lost three top clients this year, why? Were there common themes you need to address?
- If you never built an audience around your podcast—why? What got in your way?

Set your feelings aside and determine the facts on why you hit a roadblock. Your answers to the questions above will help you understand if your difficulties are a setback or a wall.

Often, a setback just means you need to continue to educate yourself, adjust your plan, and be willing to change yourself. And, you want to understand the resistance—why it was there, what it means, and if it matters.

> **Think of setbacks as a badge of honor. They mean you are doing something important!**
>
> **—Trisha Rae**

SIZE UP RESISTANCE

What you see isn't always what you get. How often have you heard the response to "How did it go?" be "I think everyone is on board. I didn't hear any big objections." I was on a call recently when the leader said, "I'll take silence as agreement!" Of course, that is an efficient way to run a meeting on more routine topics. Yet, in a change, you are looking for commitment and interest —not "I didn't openly disagree with you."

We've talked about the value of openly acknowledging tensions and disagreement. Many Wave Makers said that some conflict helped them decide what would work by bringing concerns out in the open. But as you assess where you are, consider resistance that may run below the surface and not be visible. Here are subtle clues that you may have unseen resistance on your hands:

- Silence from the team on a very important topic
- Change in behavior (e.g., a typically engaged or outspoken person becomes silent)
- Comments or questions that reinforce the importance of the status quo and minimize the need to ever change (And, questions can be statements in disguise!)
- An overly emotional reaction, even if not directed at you
- Consistent unavailability for an important discussion after repeated tries
- Failure to follow through on committed actions despite consistent agreement to do so

These examples aren't as direct as "I have concerns" or "That's a good idea, but I'm not ready to support this now"—productive resistance you can address. But since some resistance is unspoken, look for clues.

Resistance is typically caused by a divergence from:

- *Beliefs*: "What you are saying doesn't align with what I believe to be true"
- *Feelings*: "These changes make me feel uncertain or afraid"
- *Values*: "This goes against my values and principles"
- *Trust*: "I don't trust you as a credible voice on this topic"
- *Actions*: "Your actions don't give me confidence"

In my research and experience, I've found the most common initial resistance actually occurred under the surface. Examples included:

Beliefs—*an investor who gave positive signals to leadership but privately wasn't confident in the business case*

Feelings—*team members hesitant to give up individual perks and change how they develop software*

Values—*a leader who didn't believe in sharing the profits with anyone other than the most senior executives*

Trust—*colleagues who didn't trust input from someone less experienced, even though they had more knowledge*

Actions—*the group leader who preferred to compete with other groups and "win" rather than collaborate*

In all these cases, the wave was successful despite initial passive resistance because the Wave Maker overcame it through close collaboration and communication. But it's hard to break down resistance if you miss that it even exists. As Jonathan Morris, previous Chairman of North Texas YPO and current CEO of Titan Bank, shared, "You can start off big or small, but push the ball forward and don't let others around you keep you from making progress. Any big change will always have non-believers at first. If everyone saw that this was important to do, it would have been done already. There will always be resistance."

TIPS FOR ADDRESSING RESISTANCE

- *Ask questions & listen.* Resistance can simply be a need to be heard. Start with asking questions that show you are willing to hear input and disagreement and understand a different point of view.
- *Understand the root cause.* Consider why the resistance is there so you know what to do with it. Is it the topic, how it was shared, or the person who shared it? Explore why the resistance exists.
- *Educate.* Persuasive new information is needed before you can overcome resistance and update conventional wisdom. Identify what needs to be understood to move others forward.
- *Translate.* Share useful information in a way that is relevant to that person or group. Telling a story or an analogy can be a way to take new information and apply it.
- *Join forces.* Find the common ground for making progress. Know what others care most about and look for overlaps in your change. Identify an issue that can bring you together. For example, Wave Maker Guwan Jones's closing comment, "Let's work together on this," strikes a positive and productive note.

Don't be too comfortable with "no news is good news"—look more closely for signs of resistance. There may be subtle signals that the unspoken needs your attention.

Determine What You Can Influence

You've now looked at the situation, and it's time to separate what you can control or influence and what you can't. This lens returns to the Circle of Influence referenced in Stephen Covey's *7 Habits of Highly Effective People*,[2] a leadership classic. Covey outlines the difference between our Circle of Concern (what we care about) and the Circle of Influence (what we can affect).

Most of us focus too much time and energy outside our Circle of Influence and too much in our Circle of Concern. We worry about what we can't influence, much less control, such as the weather on the upcoming beach vacation or if they will like my presentation.

Covey notes that highly effective people think and act primarily within their Circle of Influence. They set aside those things over which they have no control and instead focus their time and energy where they can make a difference. They get to the "What can I do?" The gap can be immense between what we know and what we do. I do this exercise frequently in times of stress or when I'm worrying too much because it's a great way to mentally reset. Anytime we spend our energies on what we can't influence, much less control, it leads to frustration and disappointment. What you give attention to will also guide where you spend your energy and time.

I used to be anxious when speaking to large groups. I had thoughts of "I hope they like me" and "I hope I'm good enough." The big mental unlock for me in taming public speaking fears was to reset my thoughts on my intent and purpose—or what I could control. I started thinking different thoughts like, "I hope I help at least one person in the audience starts on their change after today," or "I want to share an idea that makes a difference for someone," and the big one—"I'm here to contribute to this group." My purpose is to educate and share. This purpose is in my control and isn't dependent upon being "good enough." This mindset change has made all the difference in how I think about public speaking, hosting a podcast, or being on an expert panel. Remember why you are there and what you control—starting with your thoughts.

Even when you have no control or direct influence, you can still answer, "What can I do?" For example, you may be disappointed if your organization selects an outside candidate for your new leader rather than the mentor you've known for years. If you ask, "What can I do to improve my likelihood of success with the new leader?" you'll come up with a long list of ideas. It may include everything from setting a time to meet her in person, learning about her background and previous company's way of working and culture, or sharing information you know she will need. Even in situations that you don't control or influence, you can still identify helpful actions.

We previously discussed the importance of accountability and that Wave Makers live in a world of "What can I do?" This question zeroes in on what you can influence or control. These questions can help you size up your setback.

1. *How credible was your idea?* I'm using a comprehensive definition of "idea." It may be a business concept, a process change, a new podcast, or a new program. This question can be one of the hardest to answer when you are attached to it. But step back and look at it more closely. Some questions to consider:
   • Did the idea matter to me?
   • What need or gap did it fill?
   • What was the real impact of your idea?
   • How much research did you do?
   • What facts guided you to the idea?
   • What experimentation or testing was done?
   • How did you know the idea was meaningful?
   • What made you believe it would work?

2. *Did you develop your Idea Circle?* This question determines if the idea gained traction *with others who want what you want.* Did you find interest in part of the idea but not all? What resonated and what didn't? This question helps you answer if it's:
   • the idea that needs to be reconsidered
   • the communication or how it was shared with others needs to change
   • the execution or implementation plan that fell short

3. *Who did you share your idea with?* Consider who you approached for their input or buy-in. What was their perspective? Did you discuss your ideas with those essential for making it work? These questions can help you determine if you have the right expert input and buy-in, as those are two separate objectives.

4. *Did you share your idea with both enthusiasm and substance?* We've already talked about the importance of marrying enthusiasm with substance. Now it's time to objectively assess your results. Let's look at two elements of this:
   • Was your content and plan substantive and clear? Did you have the facts you needed?
   • Did you share it with confidence and your unique brand of enthusiasm?

No one will be more excited than you about your new idea. You set the baseline, so if you show uncertainty about the concept, others will mirror that hesitation back to you. Confidence in an idea or wave doesn't mean you need to have all the answers—just that you believe in it, feel the change matters, and will find a way.

Storytelling is also a great way to help others connect to your idea personally. Did you connect the change to what others care about and appeal to their emotions, which builds commitment?

"Data doesn't change our behavior, our emotions do. Storytelling dynamically engages emotions and increases trust in the storyteller," writes Karen Eber in *The Perfect Story: How to Tell Stories that Inform, Influence, and Inspire.* "As you listen to stories, you gain empathy for the storyteller, particularly when sensing their vulnerability. As empathy increases, so does trust, creating more of the bonding neurochemical oxytocin to be released in your brain. Oxytocin indicates to our brain who is safe to know and be around, and who should be avoided."[3]

I viewed a setback as a badge of honor.

—**Trisha Rae**

5. *Did you have the credibility and knowledge to be the visible leader of the change?* Were you as informed as you needed to be? Did you gather the necessary expertise to develop and share your ideas? Also, a critical point in this question is "to be the visible leader." Were you the best to be upfront—the one to share and recommend the change? Would someone else have had more credibility on this topic? On a recent client project, leadership knew it would take an operational leader with in-depth business knowledge to champion their significant change in how they went to market. They tagged leaders with the most business credibility on this topic—not those with the biggest title.

Research tells us that change efforts need credible leaders and sponsors. And we see that all the time as it's often not just the message but who's sharing it. This doesn't mean it has to be the most senior or experienced person—credibility isn't based on age, gender, or level.

Influencers in social media don't have a title or level we admire, but we conclude they have insights we find interesting or valuable and that is enough.

I spoke with a recent college graduate who concluded she needed a more senior sponsor to help her ideas gain traction because she was so new to the organization and the business. If her idea was about starting a significant change inside the organization, her assessment may be accurate. She felt the change was more than she could do alone—at least now. However, it is not a reason to sit back or not take action on an issue she cares about and will help the organization. The caution here is not to hold yourself back or make assumptions that cause you to play too small or not take the lead, regardless of your age or level. Knowledge isn't dependent upon either of these criteria.

6. *How prepared were you for implementation?* This is a huge question listed here among the others. In fact, for most ideas and changes, execution is everything. Execution is what turns an idea into a real wave and an important outcome.

However, if you made it to implementation, you likely made notable progress. Of course, the "how" usually determines success. Research tells us that the majority of strategies fail at implementation. I believe this is true based on my years of working with many organizations and leaders on introducing change. Often, there isn't just one reason for the failure: implementation has many elements, and it will take an assessment to determine what worked and what didn't.

Organizations and people can create implementation conditions that make it very difficult for any waves to take hold. For example:

- *Hold up—I didn't know that's what you meant!* The most common obstacle I see is that it's easy to nod and agree when it's a concept on a slide. But it's a different ballgame when a leader later connects the idea and strategy to reality—to them individually and their team. "So, introducing AI will mean I'd have to reduce my team size by half?" or "So with the new system, I won't get the same level of support I've always gotten?" or "This means I can't make my own decisions about who I promote?" The concept becomes very real; therefore, the implementation has newfound resistance.

- *There are too many priorities.* Leaders identify 25 top, critical, super important, essential initiatives for the year. There are so many priorities that there are actually *no* priorities—just white noise. Or an entrepreneur launches three businesses simultaneously and confuses his audience and current customers. Personally, a decision to become healthy overnight and start running every day, only eating protein and vegetables and lifting weights three times a week probably means too many new priorities at one time.

- *A key leader is an idea machine.* You may have met the leader with so many ideas that they become the flavor of the hour/day/week. So, it's unclear what is an idea versus an intention to move forward. I once worked for a leader with this exact profile in a fast-paced, demanding culture. It was understood within his team that you didn't act on every idea because he might not even remember it the next day. A wise colleague who had worked with him longer coached me early on, "Give it a few days before you do anything and follow up with him to see if he was just brainstorming or if it was a true request."

- *The organization is ruled by the strategy of the day.* There are constant and dramatic changes in strategy or direction. Some leaders are addicted to the next new thing, and as a result, priorities are always just a suggestion. This can make your wave challenging because it's harder to tie it to a consistent larger purpose or traction because the unspoken view is that "this too shall pass." Individually, we can do this too by having a new personal priority of the day and never implement the change because we're off to the next new priority.

These factors affect implementation success, yet they don't have to be obstacles to progress. These conditions each require special planning to assess how to make progress when systemic, unsupportive forces are at play.

7. *What else was within your control in your wave?* Identify anything else you had control over that affected your outcome or contributed to your setback so you can factor that into your Plan B.

Don't build a bigger meal than anyone can eat.

—**Mark Benton**

Identify What's Outside Your Control

The other side of the coin is knowing what's outside your control. Identify factors that affected your progress but that you had absolutely no control or influence over. These rocks were just in your path. There are many times in life and work when we have to accept the situation won't change and move on—as hard as it may be.

List the issues that affected you but were truly outside your control. Push yourself here to be completely sure these influences *were* beyond your control.

For example, I coached a very knowledgeable and respected executive with the goal of eventually leading his division. In exploring his current behaviors and goals, he explained, "I'm more of an introvert, so I'm not that interesting or comfortable in front of big groups. I need to stick to smaller settings or written communication." As a result, he consistently asked others to step in for him in big group settings. His team interpreted his lack of visibility as a lack of interest or commitment. Yet, he was very engaging one-on-one, with a real passion for their work and the team.

He knew he had to change to reach his career goal in this highly net-worked, collaborative organization. We created small steps forward so he would get more comfortable in his own authentic way. We created a plan to progressively increase his confidence communicating in larger groups, and he worked on his speaking skills in low-risk, safe settings. He connected his reluctance and lack of visibility to his bigger goals and started looking for what he *could* do, although his first reaction was that this was out of his control as it "just wasn't who he was."

Here are a few questions to consider when looking at what's outside your control:

1. *Was timing a factor?* Timing has a significant impact on the success of any wave. If your wave appeared as your company faced a major market setback, the quality of your idea may not matter. Your funding request may not even be considered right after a major drop in business results. The timing was just off. In these situations, the quality of the idea or even the opportunity may not matter at this moment—maybe two months or a year later, but not today.

   Many entrepreneurs, especially in certain industries, were hit by recent changes in the economy. Some had to revisit their goals and priorities in a challenging market or put their plans on pause. It's the reality of business.

2. *How did financials or budget affect your progress?* Budgets and funding can be the difference between progress and a stall. Assess the effect of funding on your idea. Was funding nonexistent or too little to realize your goal? Yes, for what timeframe? And is this entirely outside of your influence?

3. *Did conflicting priorities affect your progress?* A leader told me that his idea was needed and important, but the business was growing dramatically. This success got in the way because there were other critical core business priorities. They worked tirelessly to honor current client commitments but didn't have adequate resources to take on anything new. His idea was important but in direct competition with other critical business priorities. As a result, his change was never fully considered. There was little he could do to change the circumstances at that time.

Develop Your Top Five Conclusions

What does your analysis tell you? If you were a writer, what would your first paragraph be? If you were a researcher, what summary conclusions would you reach?

You'll remember that in Chapter 1, we outlined that a wave:

1. Creates an undeniable impact at the right time
2. Has a more significant purpose that engages
3. Is built upon knowledge and credibility

Now, with your researcher and reporter hat on, what does your analysis tell you about why your idea hit a wall or stalled? Learn from this information before you revise your game plan.

I recently spoke with a friend who has been dreaming of a career change into consulting. She had relevant and marketable skills, but they weren't translating into actual interviews. The lack of results started to affect her confidence. She assumed a new job must not be in the cards and was very disappointed. Together, we put on our researcher hats and looked at the facts objectively. She realized she had been too dependent on applying online and had neglected to connect with her personal and professional networks. She "didn't want to burden them by asking for help." My friend concluded she had a strong résumé and the experience to make this career change, but she hadn't engaged her personal and professional network. She decided her vision still worked, but she had to change how she executed it—even if it made her uncomfortable.

What is your assessment? When ideas don't turn into waves, it's essential to stop and ask, "What are the facts telling me?" Many of us go to an answer too quickly based on our fears, assumptions, or just fatigue. And, sometimes, when the immediate answer is "It won't work" or "I'm not the one to do it," an assessment may lead you to different conclusions. Remember, Wave Makers are both persistent and flexible. They don't give up easily, but also, they also adapt and adjust. They find the path after opening new doors, as there is usually more than one way to succeed.

Creating Plan B

Plan B isn't a failure. It's simply a new, revised approach. In my experience, we often look back and realize Plan B was the better way all along, even if we didn't initially see it. When you know that your original plan isn't working, you essentially have four options:

- Change your idea
- Change your plan
- Change you
- Pause

COVID caused many to find their Plan B in almost every profession overnight. For example, with so many people stuck at home, podcasting took off in 2020. In fact, according to data from Magellan, over 160 new brands entered the podcast market for the first time every week in 2020, and the trend accelerated throughout the year.

A Plan B that paid off was the launch of the Smartless podcast, hosted by Sean Hayes, Jason Bateman, and Will Arnett. When actors couldn't work as before—new options emerged. Hayes said, "During this stay-at-home crisis, we thought, why not ask a bunch of smart and talented people questions about the world instead of constantly bothering our spouses? We really just wanted to create an atmosphere where we can be authentically us in our humor and thirst for understanding and invite the audience to laugh and learn along with us."[4] In 2021, Amazon acquired the podcast in a multi-million-dollar deal. Their Plan B was wildly successful and beyond anything they first imagined.

Like the Smartless hosts, the most important favor you can do for yourself is to learn from a setback and ask, "What are my options now?" and "What opportunities exist now that didn't before?" Allow yourself to accept what needs to change and, most importantly, decide what you can do. How can you rethink your approach given the current situation? Are there options today that didn't exist before?

Focus on what you *can* control. When Plan A isn't producing the desired results, decide to adjust and create a new Plan B.

Wave Maker Trisha Rae, founder of Christmas is for Children, explained that she viewed setbacks as part of doing something important: "I've always subscribed to the philosophy of 'Some will. Some won't. So what? Next,' and you just move on. Keep going and go to your Plan B."

Most of us can think of situations when we were hitting our heads against the wall trying to make Plan A work when Plan B was the answer all along.

Redefine the Objective and Options

Now, it's time to return to your original objective and potentially update it. You may decide your goal hasn't changed, but your approach must be different. Or you may conclude that your goal was too aggressive and that you need to phase in your change to build traction. Step one is having a clear revised goal based on what you know now that you didn't know then—based on facts, not emotion.

As we discussed previously, options can quickly put everything in perspective. An initially unattractive option can look much better when compared with the other options. Options are very powerful because they remind us that we *do* have choices. Also, options are a great way to contrast and compare to make a better decision.

Look at your options. There is never just one answer.

—Tory Johnson

For example, Ellen wanted to start a travel vlog to supplement her income and eventually be her primary income. Her career was previously in Finance in large organizations, so this goal was a very big change for her, but travel is her passion. She created a few vlogs on recent trips, but she wasn't getting much interest. She wondered if this dream was going to work. She sat down with a trusted friend and began to develop options for what to do next. They came up with:

1. Determine if your heart and values fully align with your wave.
2. Ask trusted friends, family, or colleagues to give her unbiased feedback on her videos.
3. Look at other successful travel vlogs and assess what works for them. You won't want to do what they do—but you may see an example that helps you.
4. Get advice on how to build and grow an audience. Look to see if she is missing important knowledge of how to grow her business.
5. Change how she approaches her vlogs. Explore new topics and research what topics interest her core audience. Consider the length, her destinations, and her focus.
6. Hire a marketing person. Find an expert to help her reach a bigger audience.
7. Engage more with others. Connect more with others on social media and with her network. Contribute to others' ideas and successes and actively participate in groups that love travel.
8. Stop vlogging. What started as a joy is now becoming a frustration, so she could take a pause and decide if this is more a hobby than her work.

Since Ellen's goal was to become a successful travel vlog host, she had to choose the best option based on that goal. She finally concluded that she could improve her content, but it wasn't the main thing holding her back. Her biggest obstacle was standing back and waiting for recognition and engagement to come to her. Her limited personal connections with others, especially on social media, meant her share circle was too small, so her community wasn't growing. She decided to put her energy into option #7 along with guidance from experts.

Options based on what's within your control can help you decide on a plan to address what you learned in your mini-assessment.

Create Your Plan B

Like Ellen, now that you have looked at your options and what is in your control, it's time to decide on your Plan B and take action. Plan B isn't a failure but a more educated attempt at your goal. It may even be a minor adjustment to your original plan. We know Wave Makers have adaptable persistence and find a better way.

I felt one of my most significant work disappointments on a late flight home from New York. After months of work, my team and I presented important recommendations to the executive team on significant but needed workforce changes. The business case was sound and extremely well-researched. It was packaged in a compelling way, and we'd held many pre-meetings to confirm we had the buy-in of several leaders. We presented our recommendations confidently and persuasively—we thought. We even had visible support in the room, with many nodding heads. However, one influential senior leader had limited availability for preview discussions, yet her power and force overshadowed everyone else's that day.

As the meeting progressed, I thought we were confirming our needed support. I even began to mentally prepare for questions on our next steps once we had the approval to continue. Our presentation represented almost a year of work, and I could see and feel the positive impact I knew this decision would have. Then, this senior leader stood up, and in angry and colorful language, she said, "This is not how we do things in this organization," and she was adamantly opposed to it. Period. No discussion. It shut down the room and the project. Even though other leaders agreed with our recommendations, they stayed silent on that day.

What I didn't know at the time was that her line in the sand actually built support with others on the executive team. They had bought into the change even though she hadn't. It took breaking the plan into two pieces and going at it again, but within a year, the program was fully introduced with some minor tweaks. It was a significant change, and I don't think it would have happened without the pain of trying to get approval for Plan A. Plan B eventually carried the day—just not on my original timing.

Plan B needs a nice balance of optimism and reality. On one end of the spectrum, you have some of the most amazing innovators of all time, including Steve Jobs, Jeff Bezos, and Thomas Edison, who ignored the naysayers and moved their dreams forward when no one else could even imagine it. At the other end is the person who is overly responsive to feedback, changing the plan with every new conversation he has. Find the balance for your work and situation.

The critical lesson in conducting your diagnostic and developing your options is to learn from setbacks and disappointments. Spend your energy on what is in your control. After time to think and analyze, your Plan B will emerge and may even be stronger than your first idea. And realize that Plan B may also evolve into C, D, or E. Stay fluid and adaptable while also staying persistent toward your ultimate goal.

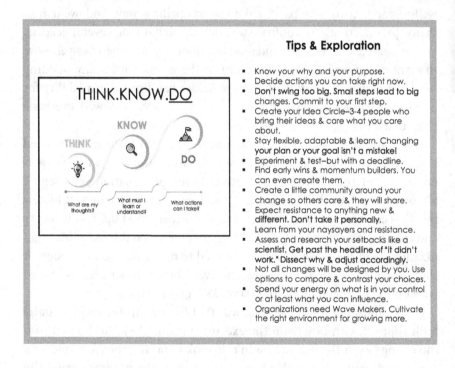

THINK TIME

You've gone through your diagnostic and have ideas on what to do next and your Plan B. That is your goal—decide what's next.

1. What is your Plan B?
2. What will you do differently this time?
3. What good ideas should be saved for later but not utilized at this time?
4. What can you do now to adjust and adapt to your revised approach?
5. Who else will be part of it with you? Are there differences from when you began?
6. What are the key milestones in your plan to move you forward?

NOTES

1 Kim Holcomb interviewer, Clooney Visits University of Washington to Promote 'Boys in the Boat' (NBC K5 Interview, 2024).
2 Stephen Covey, *7 Habits of Highly Effective People* (New York: Simon & Schuster, updated 2020).
3 Karen Eber, *The Perfect Story* (Nashville, TN: Harper Horizon, 2023).
4 Natalie Jarvey, *Hollywood Reporter*, July 2020.

Part 4

Other Things to Think About

9

Why Leaders Need More Wave Makers

The main idea behind *Make Waves* is that anyone can start a wave or a significant change. Anyone. Innovative and growing organizations need these grassroots ideas, changes, and experimentation to reach their goals.

Fresh thinking and new ideas are essential for any successful organization.

Leaders can't possibly know the answers to everything in this complex and changing world. It's just not possible. They need you. Successful changes have contributions from individuals who made an immeasurable impact because of their wave. Individuals like you who ask, "What can I do?" or "What if?"

Rich Sheridan took the importance of everyone's contribution to heart across the entire Menlo Innovations organization. Menlo Innovations disregards many of the standard business practices, such as a reliance on traditional hierarchy. The change to that flattened structure took commitment from everyone, not just a few top leaders. Menlo is built on paired working and high collaboration, with an empathetic approach. High-Tech Anthropologists®, the name Menlo has for its developers, have a lofty, self-stated goal: to end human suffering in the world as it relates to technology™.

The team at Menlo Innovations has a fresh take on most aspects of running a business. For example, Menlo's hiring process is called "Extreme Interviewing." It feels almost like speed dating. Applicants come to the office for a series of fast-paced interviews with several current employees. The employees look for "kindergarten skills," such as geniality, curiosity, and generosity. The Menlo view of Extreme Interviewing is that technical proficiency is less important than a candidate's "ability to make [his or her] partner look good."

DOI: 10.4324/9781032715339-13

After the interviews, the Menlonians involved gather to make some decisions. They argue, debate, and lobby one another. After a healthy discussion, interviewers rank candidates on their technical skills and also on what they term the "value set" of cultural fit. Based on the evaluation, offers are extended to the applicants at the top of the list. One leader can't override everyone, nor do the most senior leader and the HR and Recruiting experts decide. The decision is completely made by other team members.

Like the team at Menlo Innovations, I believe we are all leaders and contributors. Some lead hundreds of people or an entire organization, while others lead themselves and the work they do each day. Regardless of your position, you are essential in encouraging waves from your team, peers, and partners.

BENEFITS OF WAVE MAKERS

Organizations depend upon stability and repeatability to complete key processes effectively and deliver results. But there is a difference between leading and managing. Leading creates change and movement, and management produces consistent results. Wave Makers are the ones who look for a better way, explore possibilities, see new ideas, and avoid the complacency of familiarity. Wave Makers serve as human catalysts for change and growth.

Leaders need Wave Makers because they:

Spark Innovation

As we discussed above, innovation comes from individuals with new and relevant ideas. Great organizations need innovation in different ways and on various topics. Leaders can give inspiring presentations on the importance of innovation, but the hard part is connecting that philosophy to everyone who works there, not just the head of strategy or the chief innovation officer. Everyone can contribute to innovation and strategic change.

As FCEB member Solomon Thimothy, president and founder of OneIMS, said, "While it's always important to anticipate and mitigate risk, a forward-thinking company encourages experimentation and risk-taking. An innovative business is willing to reorganize, restructure, or rethink to best serve the forward motion of the organization. We need more of those who are willing to challenge the status quo. Those who constantly push themselves to experience uniqueness and are willing to redefine what's been set as a limit."[1]

Wave Maker Lois Melbourne, cocreator and former CEO of Aquire, shared the connection between risk and innovation and creating a culture that encourages waves: "I think it's respect. You've got to respect people for taking the risk. You have to give them the ability to fail and not take a hit for their failures. Look at what worked and what didn't and learn from both. If an organization respects outside thought, then anyone can say, 'Let's try this.' Encourage 'skunkworks,' risk-taking, and exploration. Fear is anti-innovation."

> **If someone tries something and it fails, then let it fail gracefully and not with fear.**
>
> —**Lois Melbourne**

Elevate Performance

It is amazing how two or three Wave Makers can raise performance in a team. Positive peer pressure can cause others to step up, too. A few years ago, I experienced the impact of a recent college graduate on a client team that had been doing their work the same way for years. This recent graduate didn't judge or criticize, but she started a change in that team without a big campaign to do so. She started using new technology to streamline and improve access to meaningful data and made suggestions on work processes once she understood the goals. Her actions started to change how the team worked, and she raised the bar for the entire team's performance. And she was smart in the way she did it. She focused on the work, not the judgment of those who did it.

Accelerate Talent Development

Hands down, one of the best ways to accelerate your personal and professional development is to work on a new idea or a change. You can't rely on a process or the last version to tell you how it must be done. This work requires a fresh perspective and new ideas. No prescribed road map tells you where to go.

When I think of my waves—creating a new service line, starting a business, publishing a book, and exploring the acquisition of our company. I had moments of fear and wondered how I'd get through it in each of these situations. All produced big changes for me and our teams and these were my most significant high-growth periods. I learned so much in these years that helped me leapfrog my knowledge and insights.

One of my clients has created a career plan that includes what they call "critical experiences." These are defined as experiences that accelerate an employee's development, increase capabilities, and, in turn, help the business. Changes can provide a critical experience across almost any type of work. Waves are ideal for career and capability acceleration.

Shake Up the Status Quo

If you or your leaders feel the organization has gotten too stale and needs an influx of new ideas, then a Wave Maker can help. A colleague just accepted a CHRO role. As she explained her decision to take the opportunity, she said, "They want to shake up their status quo and need a new perspective. I know I'll have my challenges coming in with the expectation to drive change—but the idea of a blank slate to re-invent is so exciting." Their hiring decision was a strategic move to hire a Wave Maker and bring in change.

Any new change requires debate and discussion. Yet, the status quo is the only option that is not usually debated. It's the choice that becomes the favorite option without a decision ever actually being made. Every group needs people thinking about the next big thing: how to improve work and improve our quality of life. You need people who can provide fresh alternatives to the status quo.

ENCOURAGING WAVE MAKERS

Wave Makers are cultivated through encouragement, acknowledgment, and being valued. Organizations can send cultural messages that keep aspiring change-makers on the sidelines. You won't nourish Wave Makers if you punish failure or if there is a career penalty for being wrong or not agreeing with the boss. If you want to encourage change and new ideas, the following strategies work.

Welcome New Ideas

It seems apparent that you should welcome new ideas if you want to change things, but this point is often missed. This strategy is not just a feel-good move; it's essential for collaboration and innovation, assuming those offering the ideas have the insight and knowledge to back them up. I have been in many leadership conversations about a business challenge or a broken process that needed to change. You hope that executive-level meetings aren't the first stop for these conversations. What do those closest to the work have to say? Some of the best ideas for change come from those who truly understand the work.

We talked earlier about the power of back-of-the-napkin conversations and not already having the answer when you show up. This is true whether you are leading a change or large organization. Encourage others who have the knowledge and capability to contribute.

You can also ask questions to your team and colleagues that signal you are open to a new way. Questions like:

- *How could we make this better?*
- *What ideas from other industries are relevant to us?*
- *What can we do in one to three years to re-invent this?*
- *What are we missing?*

Leaders must set expectations for the timing of new ideas. Sometimes, ideas must pause because you are implementing the ideas you decided upon last month. Unless a business reason says the idea won't work or needs to be revisited, save it until the next version or upgrade. Melisa Miller of Alliance Data focused her organization on contributing ideas where they were needed, but she didn't ask for ideas on the critical business outcomes that were already established. Those weren't up for debate, and that was understood.

Likewise, filter ideas before we share them. You have probably seen a person who is spilling over with ideas. Rather than influencing others, they share any and all ideas with others without prequalification for value, relevance, or alignment with goals.

I spoke to a friend recently about my book, and this topic came up. She mentioned someone on her team with great ideas on a ratio of about 1:10—one great idea for every ten shared. If you stayed with him, you'd eventually hear a few great ideas, but it would take time, patience, and filtering through a lot of irrelevant information. Time and patience that most aren't willing to give. My friend advised him that ideas must be more than just top-of-mind thoughts unless it's a rapid-fire generation discussion. Create the opportunity to hear new ideas and also keep your ideas relevant and impactful.

Encourage Experimentation

To encourage means to support, hope for, and enable. As I shared earlier, experimentation is vital to any change. What happens when we experiment? Some things work, and some don't. Our hypothesis is tested. Experiments provide information we didn't know before. Start small and see what works. So, "encourage experimentation" implies that not everything will work.

As Rick Rubin, the legendary music producer, shares in *The Creative Act: A Way of Being*, "Perhaps take on the temporary rule that there are no bad ideas. Test them all even the ones that seem underwhelming or unlikely to work. This method becomes especially useful in group efforts. Often when working with others, different ideas are put forward and end up in competition. Based on experience, we may believe we can see what each person is imagining and what the result will be." Rubin adds, "When working thorough ways of solving a puzzle, there are no mistakes. Each unsuccessful solution gets you closer to one that works."[2]

Some leaders say they encourage experimentation, yet there is no tolerance when something goes wrong. I distinguish between an experiment that didn't work and a mistake made because a process wasn't followed or a customer problem went unaddressed. The latter differs from deliberate experimentation, which naturally includes problems and mistakes.

Make Room for Others to Lead

Let others lead the experiment or try a new idea. Leaders often believe that having all the answers is a key ingredient for respect and success. We know that inviting others to be part of starting and creating a change is essential for innovation and starting a wave. Leaders must be willing to step to the sidelines and let others be visible, make important decisions, and lead the effort.

One of the most impressive executives I worked for was masterful at being in charge when needed and stepping back so others could lead, too. He often encouraged those with great ideas to share and test their ideas and gave them some limited funding or support. These simple acts showed how much he valued new ideas and the input of others.

I'm not recommending an abdication of leadership, and many situations call for a leader to visibly lead the change. But, if your goal is to encourage broader participation and encourage others to safely bring their ideas, you have to share the stage. This is even more essential in the community because volunteers have total freedom and choice in how they spend their time.

Listen Well

We've discussed listening throughout *Make Waves*. Listening is always essential, and it's vital for encouraging Wave Makers. The absolute first step in engaging with someone who wants to start a change is listening. Most of the Wave Makers I interviewed started with, "I have an idea. What do you think?"

Listening is one of the ways you signal you are interested in new ideas. If you don't practice good listening skills, you send signals you already know everything you need to know. You will get your wish if you communicate—even unintentionally—that no new ideas are needed here. We know that ignoring new information is a weakness when navigating through any change.

Recognize and Reward Wave Making

Changes aren't your standard project or initiative. There will inevitably be bumps and ongoing adjustments. There may not be immediate success. Most changes take time, so stay persistent and set aside your ego. This mindset doesn't fit the conventional wisdom on fast-tracking a career. However, many Wave Makers felt that starting their change profoundly impacted their growth and success.

Bruce Ballengee started Pariveda Solutions to create a different organization, including how contribution is recognized and rewarded.

Bruce recalled the early discussions of starting the business: "We'll do consulting, but it has to be interesting. We want to think about our industry differently—with a new business model. Our model will be almost inverted from the traditional business model. On the surface, they don't look that different. But you get underneath the covers, and it's really different, and that's what makes it interesting and very challenging at multiple levels."

Leaders can enable changes with more than just encouragement. The proof comes when executives visibly and wholeheartedly recognize those who step out. Consider behaviors and decisions that will stop any promising Wave Makers:

- Do you subtly penalize those who led an experiment that didn't work?
- Do you brand those with new ideas as too ambitious or not knowing their place?
- Do you rely on hierarchy and wonder why an analyst shared her ideas rather than letting her director be the one to speak up?
- Do you withhold a promotion or salary increase for those who achieved success in nontraditional ways?

It won't matter what you say if you don't formally and informally reward and recognize those who start and make changes.

DEVELOPING WAVE MAKERS

Wave Makers don't just appear in every culture or organization. Some seem to intuitively know how to think creatively, be bold, or see the unseen. This "change brain" can be developed with the right experiences and environment. Let's look at ideas for creating the capability needed to help others become a Wave Maker.

Bruce Ballengee, Wave Maker and CEO of Pariveda Solutions said that he views his purpose and that of the organization as teaching and developing. He is a big advocate of active mentoring, which he says is one of the things he enjoys most about his work. Bruce said, "The best part of my work is developing talented people from the time they join after college to when they reach their potential in this organization. I really like teaching, and Pariveda is really a platform to teach and help others learn. I have a lot of fun teaching other people, including a very early exposure to the idea of growing relationships and helping others—paying it forward."

Ask Questions That Teach

We know waves are often developed not because of creative genius but because of asking insightful questions. These questioners have a habit of exploring and being curious about why and how. As a leader, one of the ways you can develop others to start changes is by asking them questions and helping them learn to ask the same questions themselves.

At Accenture, I worked for a wise leader, Don Monaco, who typically responded to recommendations with, "Walk me through your thinking," "What alternatives did you consider?" "Why did you choose this option?" "What outcomes can we expect if we do this?" and "What will it cost?" His questions taught me a lot about the thought process for ideas that will work. He ingrained this thinking into his team, so we learned to ask ourselves these questions while bringing forth new ideas. And you can, too, even if your leaders don't ask.

Give "White Space" Assignments

White space is my way of saying the work is not fully defined, and shaping is needed to develop the change. In these times, there is no precedent or clear road map to follow. The objective may be known, but no design has been created. And the exact outcome may not even be known yet—just the problem.

In these scenarios, it's up to the individuals involved to create what doesn't exist today using research, insights, and instinct. One of my "go-to" questions when I want to understand and individual's ability to design and create is, "How effective are they with a blank space?" It's another way of asking if that person can thrive with no boundaries or roadmap—only a goal or outcome.

At Accenture, I had the opportunity to work on acquisitions or consolidations in new markets and businesses. Even though I was in a well-established consulting firm, some of my projects made me feel like I was working at a start-up because we created completely new strategies, cultures, plans, and processes for these new businesses. These experiences are what we joked at the time were "career dog years"—when you get seven years of experience all rolled into one because everything was new and hard. Even so, these experiences were a true difference-maker for me.

Leaders can plan these assignments to build Wave Maker capabilities. And we can each seek out these types of assignments to develop our capability as well. This experience in the white space helps everyone who can handle it.

Put People Out of Their Zone

We all have zones that fit our expertise, where we are most comfortable and confident. Have you ever noticed that when a new person comes in, they often have an observation or insight that those working there for months missed? Someone with a fresh perspective can see what others can't. They aren't necessarily wiser; they just don't have the blinders that come after looking at something too long.

In writing this book, I have asked friends and colleagues to read and give me their thoughts. I recently told a friend, "I've looked at this for so long; sometimes, I can't see it anymore." We see how others can solve their problems much more quickly than we can solve our own.

You can develop future Wave Makers by proactively looking for stretch roles and assignments they can take. It's not setting up someone to fail but asking them to take on a stretch role or project. This experience helps your people expand their horizons and see the world differently.

While no one told me to start my business, I decided to jump in. It was out of my zone at first, and I felt some anxiety as a result. While the work content was familiar, how it was delivered and all the responsibilities that come with starting a new business were completely new and a little scary. I had come from a huge organization with tools, support, and access to almost anything. I have to laugh now as I reflect on some of my naïve beliefs and assumptions at the beginning. Starting my business was a process of developing my strengths and weaknesses and changing my perspective on more issues than I could count.

Promote Wider Thinking

In bigger organizations, it's easy to slip into roles and teams that are isolated from others. Silos are one of the most common business problems in general, which makes change, innovation, and collaboration a real challenge. Leaders need organizational groups to deliver on their promises and commitments, but not when the group becomes more important than the larger goal.

In organizations like McKesson, Amazon, and PepsiCo, it is common to ask high-potential leaders to take on a role that expands their business knowledge or brings their experience to a new space. A client wanted to crack the code on making Diversity, Inclusion, and Belonging part of how they run their business rather than a separate corporate initiative. Surprisingly, they selected a business leader to redefine the function as they saw her operational knowledge as essential for approaching this strategic priority differently.

Asking individuals to lead a project beyond their role and function naturally expands thinking. It also causes them to understand the needs of other organizational groups through firsthand experience. It's a great way to gain perspective and see the business and the market differently.

EDUCATE ON HOW TO START A CHANGE

My main goal in writing *Make Waves* is to provide ideas, encouragement, and insights for those who want to start a wave. There are strategies, habits, and actions that will increase your chances of creating a sustainable wave. While some use these strategies naturally and by instinct, I absolutely believe they can be learned.

There are Wave Makers all around us—some work in big organizations, and others in small ones. Others are entrepreneurs. Some are in their twenties; others have retired and created a second career. Some started big-scale changes, and others started with a pebble that made lasting ripples and turned into something bigger. With all of their differences, there were patterns and similarities because all were starting a change. The pattern tells us there is something there to learn. The ability to start a change isn't something you were born with but can be learned.

If you educate yourself and develop the skills needed to start and sustain a change, the likelihood of being able to repeat it increases dramatically. You probably have people in your organization who meet this profile today. You likely don't call them Wave Makers, but you know who they are.

As I said in Chapter 1, when I asked trusted friends and colleagues for their Wave Makers, they all quickly understood and shared their examples.

Ensure that those who have made waves in your organization share and help build that capability in others. And recognize them!

LEADERS AND WAVE SPONSORSHIP

If you start a bigger wave inside an organization, you will likely need sponsorship at some point. Look for those who are in a position to support, sponsor, or connect. If your change needs a sponsor in your organization, zero in on precisely what you need to determine who can best help you. You may need funding, expertise, or someone who can influence others. Sponsorship is always essential, but you must know what kind of sponsorship you need.

Likewise, if you advocate for Wave Makers, determine how to best offer your support. Here are a few types of sponsors that Wave Makers may need:

Advocate: The Advocate is behind you and the effort and will tell anyone about the importance of your change. They are in your corner privately and publicly. Advocates usually see your change as aligned with a broader vision or strategy they support, personally or organizationally.

Connector: The Connector is a role leaders can play inside or outside an organization. When I started my business, I had many Connectors who said, "You should know…" and they made that introduction happen. Also, leaders can champion grassroots efforts inside their organization and help Wave Makers connect with other sponsors who can help.

Validator: The Validator is the expert who confirms that your idea is sound and that you have considered all relevant issues. The Validator can add credibility to your idea or change by giving it a stamp of approval, even if they aren't actively involved.

Funder: The funder provides the resources (typically money or people) you need to get started, experiment, or engage others. Inside an organization, it is the person who controls the budget. If you are an entrepreneur, it may be an investor who funds your idea or new business. A Connector may help you get a funder or a funding source.

Advisor: The advisor may not be a visible supporter, but he provides wise guidance and mentoring as needed. The advisor is a sponsor who has typically accomplished a relevant goal and is well-qualified to help you strategize and consider options. Sometimes, advisors may also be other types of sponsors, though not always. I have had many advisors in my career who offered valued wisdom and counsel even when not visibly involved in the work.

If you are a leader in a position to sponsor a change, remember to ask Wave Makers, "What role can I play? How can I be helpful to you?" This type of advocacy from leaders powers the grassroots efforts and experiments. Likewise, if you want to start a wave, identify the types of sponsors you need.

Leaders everywhere can decide to be difference makers and help needed changes to see the light of day. Determine the sponsors you need to make your wave happen, then work to get them involved.

THINK TIME

1. How can Wave Makers make your organization or community better?
2. How can you encourage Wave Makers on your team or within your organization? What obstacles exist today that need to be addressed?
3. What actions can you take for yourself and your team to develop the skills and knowledge needed to be a Wave Maker?
4. What kind of sponsors do you need to realize your wave? Who can play this role for you?
5. What kind of sponsor can you be for others as they pursue their changes and goals?

NOTES

1 Fast Company Executive Board, "Innovation in Business: 5 Characteristics of an Innovative Company."
2 Rick Rubin, *The Creative Act: A Way of Being* (New York: Penguin Press, 2023), pp. 138–139.

10

Wisdom from Wave Makers

I asked Wave Makers for their encouragement and ideas for how to reach your goals and make your changes a reality.

WHAT YOU THINK

- *How you think will have the most impact on your success. Start there.*
- *Trust your passion, not your ego.*
- *It's ok if you don't know how to do it yet. But, start with the belief of "I can figure this out."*
- *It will be difficult, fraught with problems and risks. If it doesn't work out, it will be OK. You still did the right thing. You've fulfilled a large part of your potential by doing that. You get more than one chance.*
- *Have a clear vision even if it changes over time.*
- *It takes courage to have patience. It's important because real change takes time.*
- *If you have a dream, you've got to get moving, or it's never going to happen.*
- *You need to choose to do it first—and then find a way to get it done.*
- *Learn to feel comfortable with ambiguity. In most situations, roughly right is ok.*
- *Be confident in what you're doing. Don't be afraid of what other people will think of you.*
- *Keep it simple. Don't overwork the small things that aren't important to your bigger goals. This way, you can spend your energy on what matters most.*

DOI: 10.4324/9781032715339-14

- Grow your resiliency muscle because you'll need it time and time again.
- Give your gifts along the way—your time, your ideas, and your empathy.

WHAT YOU KNOW

- Accept that you can't already know everything you need to know. It's a new change—it's impossible. Don't let your ego or fear of not knowing keep you from learning.
- Don't squash resistance. Use that knowledge as power. Be open to feedback and listen. Fully understanding your resistance is powerful. Then you know what you're facing.
- Make sure you have both a great idea and a need. You need both.
- Learn as much as you can, but after that, it will come down to you deciding what to do.
- Even if you are knowledgeable on a topic, continue to seek out new information and ideas. Every situation is different.
- Have evidence that supports your view.
- Look outside your own world and at what other industries and companies are doing—even if their situation is different from yours. Look for new, interesting ideas and find their relevance in your world.
- No change is perfect. Ever. So, don't set that expectation.

WHAT YOU DO

- Get others involved in your change and vision early. Most people vastly underestimate how much time and work getting people involved in the change takes.
- Listen to others. Treat everyone with respect even if you disagree.
- Get approvals in baby steps if that's what it takes. Find a way to get started and make progress
- Have a little core group. If you are doing this by yourself, it can be very lonely and very hard.

- *Use the decision maker's own words and phrases in your request. It will be harder to resist!*
- *You don't get what you don't ask for. You don't have to ask for the world. Be an incrementalist. You can always go back for more.*
- *Allow time to commit to this. Remember things don't happen overnight. One of the biggest obstacles is that people abandon ship too soon.*
- *The best way to get people on board is by feeling they have a piece in it.*
- *Give before you get.*
- *Learn to pace yourself and be realistic. You can't always do the ideal, but still keep going. The best you can do at that moment is ok and it matters*
- *You can't take resistance personally. It's usually not about you.*
- *Encouragement is powerful, and anyone can do it.*
- *Know the difference between starting something and owning it.*
- *Be prepared that not everything is going to turn out just right. That doesn't mean your overall strategy is off, just because one tactic was. Learn, course correct, and stay with it.*

Index

Printed in the United States
by Baker & Taylor Publisher Services

Printed in the United States
by Baker & Taylor Publisher Services